SASHIKO

Blue and White Quilt Art of Japan

Kazuko Mende and Reiko Morishige

First printing, 1991

Book design by Momoyo Nishimura
English Text supervised by Jane Singer

Published by Shufunotomo Co., Ltd.,
2-9, Kanda Surugadai, Chiyoda-ku,
Tokyo, 101 Japan

DISTRIBUTORS
United States: Kodansha America, Inc.,
through Farrar, Straus & Giroux,
19 Union Square West, New York, NY 10003.
Canada: Fitzenry & Whiteside Ltd.,
195 Allstate Parkway, Markham, Ontario L3R 4T8.
British Isles & European Continent: Premier Book
Marketing Ltd.,
1 Gower Street, London WC1E 6HA.
Australia and New Zealand: Bookwise International,
54 Crittenden Road, Findon, South Australia 5023.
The Far East and Japan: Japan Publications Trading Co.,
1-2-1, Sarugaku-cho, Chiyoda-ku, Tokyo 101.

Printed in Japan
ISBN 0-87040-828-3

Contents

Textiles:
Designed by Kazuko Mende
Made by Reiko Morishige

PREFACE

The word "indigo" in Japanese evokes special feelings—of both fondness and nostalgia—among many Japanese people.

Indigo is actually the name of a plant. First introduced to Japan from ancient Egypt via China at around the third century A.D., it has been cultivated as a source of dye since then. Cotton dyed in indigo is strong; warm in winter, cool in summer and rarely moth-eaten, it became popular throughout Japan during the Edo period (1603–1867). But while the dyed fabric itself needed little care initially, extracting the dye from the plant was quite a troublesome and time-consuming task, and it took more effort than for other natural dyes to keep indigo in usable condition.

The life cycle of indigo dye is said to resemble that of a human being. In the beginning, indigo in a pot is pale in color. As it matures, it becomes darker in color, until it ends its life as a dye. Like man, indigo is born, grows, matures and ages. In fact, according to a Japanese saying, nursing a pot of indigo is as difficult as bringing up a child. Although today our work is made easier by the existence of chemical dyes colored indigo, the dye extracted from the indigo plant is still highly valued.

The pattern craft called "sashiko" was originally employed to make sturdy, warm work-clothes. In order to clothe their husbands in outfits that were both warm and strong, the wives of farmers and fishermen sewed together two or more pieces of fabric and lovingly adorned them with original designs. These patterns were passed on to later generations, and their use eventually spread throughout Japan.

Today, indigo-dyed cloth and sashiko are no longer in common everyday use, but these hand-crafted fabrics have gained appeal as stylish wear and for interior decoration, especially for people who value traditional dress.

Using such traditional materials as indigo-dyed cloth, and through the use of the simple technique of sashiko, we have fashioned artistic works which suit contemporary lifestyles. Since 1980, when we began explaining our work to non-Japanese after holding shows in Tokyo and New York, we naturally had to explain also about traditional Japanese patterns. Although we have not consciously imitated traditional Japanese folk art, we have become aware of the traditional aspects that can be found in our work.

In this book, we would like you to understand our work as being rooted in the history of Japanese folk art—as products of the Japanese environment and Japanese ideas of beauty. In our explanations of various patterns, we have included comments about Japanese aesthetics and the influential art works of the past.

Kazuko Mende
Reiko Morishige

JAPANESE PATTERNS

Kazuko Mende

The term "ornamentation" refers to figures and patterns intended to beautify objects.

Ornaments never stand on their own; they always rely on a foundation. Ornamentation is said to be a solution to man's intrinsic fear of emptiness and his need to fill vacuums. Thus, man has valued ornamentation since primitive times, and has employed decorative patterns which reflect the tastes and values of the day.

Most figures and patterns are simplified representations of man's view of nature and the world, shaped and ordered within boundaries. Among Japanese figures one can find a variety of designs, some modeled on real objects, others symbolic of natural phenomena.

Some figures are composed like a painting, but *Emoyo* "patterns" usually refer to graphic shapes which could be used alone as decoration or could be composed of repetitions of figures. Yet, while a pattern evolves from a graphic form, it is quite different in nature from fine art, which can be seen as a pure expression of man's essence. While fine art tends to be individual expression, patterns develop from common feelings and world views.

Forms which are combined into a symbolic pattern or those with a specific meaning are often called *Mon* (crests). These include family crests, highly abstract and refined symmetrical patterns which date from the Kamakura period (12th century), and are modeled after plants, animals, natural phenomena, tools, geometric shapes and characters.

White with Twill Weave Grapevine Patterns. Nara period, 8th century. The Shosoin Collection, Nara.

There are innumerable patterns in the world, and each is intimately linked with the culture of the area from which it came. For example, designs of lush branches and fruit-bearing vines were used as pattern motifs in Persia, where vines were indigenous to the culture. In Rome, vines were replaced by acanthus, and in China, where grapes were not grown in abundance, the *Karakusa mon* (arabesque design) was formed, modeled on different kinds of plants, combined with figures of birds. Some patterns are common all around the world, such as *Shima-monyo* (stripes) and *Koshi-monyo* (checks), but they are thought to have developed from different roots and carry different meanings. The Scottish Tartan checks, for instance, resemble the Japanese *Benkeijima* of *benkeigoshi* (checked pattern) in form, but the meaning is completely different. Based on this assumption that "figures" and "patterns" reflect their specific regions and historical periods, we can explore the historical development of Japanese patterns.

PATTERNS OF THE PREHISTORIC ERA

The most common decorative patterns of the Jomon and Yayoi periods (B.C. 10th C–B.C. 4th C) were designs on earthenware surfaces. Jomon earthenware is known for patterns made by pressing a thin rope against the surface of the earthenware. Other patterns were produced by using shells or bamboo to incise or fill in the spaces in the surface of earthenware, but these were always limited to simple geometric patterns.

During the Yayoi period, *Sugiaya-moyo* (herringbone patterns) and *Koshi-monyo* (checked patterns) began to appear on earthenware, and *Uzumaki-mon* (spirals) and *Ryusui-mon* (running water patterns) were seen on copper bells. Although the base material differs, one could say that the repetitive patterns of the Yayoi were inherited from the Jomon period. Pictorial art also began to appear during the Yayoi period. As figures of man and animals were sometimes drawn within the outline of geometric patterns, they could be seen as some type of spiritual symbol. It seems that man first created tools, then adorned them to embue the tools with spritual meaning.

PATTERNS IN ANCIENT TIMES

Patterns have lyrical as well as narrative aspects. Patterns in the prehistoric period were used to demonstrate respect for the gods in nature. Later, patterns expressing human feelings begin to appear. This chapter introduces patterns in the dynastic eras, including the Hakuho period (645–710 A.D.), Nara period (710–794) and Heian period (794–1192).

Cultural exchanges between China and Korea were already active by the end of the fifth century, and Buddhism was introduced from Korea to Japan in the Asuka period (late sixth century to seventh century). At that time, many immigrants to Japan who had been saddle makers began applying their skills to sculpting Buddhist idols. The ornamentation of the

Genji Monogatari Emaki (picture scroll of the Tale of Genji) Inks and colors on paper. Heian period, early 12th century.

Nindo-karakusa-mon (palmette patterns) on the forms of Buddha during that period indicates the passion and technical mastery of these sculptors. The influence of Chinese-Korean culture can be clearly seen in the *Renge-mon* (lotus flower patterns) of the roof tiles in temples dating from the Hakuho period, as well as in the *Budo-karakusa-mon* (arabesque with vine pattern), the *Shishin-mon* (Four-Gods pattern) and the *Renju-mon* (pearl motif pattern) decorating the dais under the three famous statues found in Nara's Yakushiji Temple (*Yakushiji-sanzon-shumidan*).

The patterns and designs that were popular in periods after the Asuka era can be found in the Shosoin Repository in Nara. The Shosoin's collection of art treasures begins with items used in the con-secration ceremony of the *Daibutsu* (Great Buddha) held in 752, and the personal belongings of Emperor Shomu, which were donated by his wife in 756. A great body of other items are kept in the Shosoin, and as they have rarely been displayed, most are in excellent condition.

Today, a small part of the collection is exhibited to the public once a year. The treasures range from Buddhist items to utensils of emperors and aristocrats: incense, medicine, dyes, ancient documents and even census rolls of common people. These objects reveal highly civilized, artistically splendid ancient cultures. They also include many imported goods, or copies of these items, which originated in Tang-dynasty China, Central Asia, Persia and Byzantine. All kinds of patterns can be found in the Shosoin col-

From *Hahakigi*, second section of painting. Original handscroll, 15 sections of scenes and 28 sections of text. The Tokugawa Art Museum, Aichi.

lection, but a common and distinctive feature is the combination of animal and plant patterns. Japanese design patterns reflect the culture's traditional agricultural values. Besides a few species of birds, animals are rarely depicted. Yet the animals depicted in the collection include lions, elephants, camels, rhinoceros, deer, peacocks and parrots, none of which are found in Japan. Plants include coconut and banana and other tropical trees unknown to Japan, which no Japanese designer could have drawn. Also, there is evidence that the vine pattern, which originated in Persia and came to China via the Silk Road, was probably introduced to Japan in the form of wine glasses of white lapis adorned with vines and an eight-sided elongated bowl of gold-plated copper (*Kondo-hakkyoku-chohai*) found in the Shosoin collection.

Items the Shosoin collection show that the people of the Nara period clearly merged their perceptions of the "Paradise" of Buddhist China with the idea of paradise in Persian culture. Patterns modeled on foreign subjects are laid out symmetrically or in circles, or they fill up the defined space, as if to present an image of paradise. The beautiful treasures of Shosoin reveal a strong fascination with other cultures and a desire to seek out.

During the Heian period, the practice of sending envoys, or *kentoshi,* to Tang China ceased, and patterns which had originally shown a strong Chinese influence began to become more and more Japanese. When Japan first had contact with China, Chinese rule were strongly centralized and authoritarian, supported by political theories and Confucianist ideas which emphasized well-ordered human relations. Chinese aesthetics also prized order and harmony.

Japanese aesthetics, on the other hand, emphasized religion and a love of nature. The Japanese people of this period combined their perspectives with the Chinese concept of nature, and gave birth to flower and bird motifs. As Chinese design subjects were modified according to Japanese conceptions, Heian patterns were developed with their own unique colors and compositions. In the *Genji Monogatari Emaki*, the picture scroll of The Tale of Genji, for example, each layer of the court ladies' many-layered kimono was colored differently, and each color was given the name of a seasonal plant, such as

Ume (plum), *Rindo* (gentian) and *Yamabuki* (kerria). By choosing how to layer these colors, women in the Heian period tried to express their appreciation of nature.

Such sophisticated aesthetic values suggest that the Japanese sense of color surpassed that of the Chinese. People living in these dynastic eras also began to appreciate flowers for their intrinsic beauty instead of regarding them only as an offering to Buddha, and, in general, the Japanese expression of flower and bird patterns became more refined.

MEDIEVAL PATTERNS

After the dynastic era, when aesthetic standards were set by the aristocrats in Court, the samurai class

Heiji Monogatari Emaki (Stories about the Heiji Civil War). 13th century. Tokyo National Museum.

began to assert control of art and culture. Warriors began to sport artistically decorated armor. However, the style of their armor showed the continuing influence of the aristocratic aesthetics which had been established earlier. Samurai in the *Heiji Monogatari Ekotoba* (the picture scroll of The Tales of Heiji) are seen wearing colorful and decorative armor. The armor was often decorated with designs of plants, such as oak leaves and chrysanthemums, and it was resplendent with brilliantly colored thread and leather, just like the kimono of the court ladies.

When aspects of Chinese zen culture were introduced to Japan by Zen Buddhist priests in the 14th century, they sent shock waves through Japanese society; Chinese culture became the focus of attention for the intellectuals of the day. A document detailing the interior decor used for shogunal residences, the *Kundaikan-sochoki* (A Book of Secrets), shows that interior decor was then based on Chinese aesthetics. Chinese-style landscape paintings, portraying a world of black and white, were also favored at this time, yet designs themselves became more realistic than before, to allow more individual artistic expression. Plants were portrayed realistically, in three-dimensional form, although plant motifs later became more stylized. The blossoming of Zen-influenced culture gave birth to *Chanoyu* (the tea ceremony) and fostered the veneration of Chinese Confucian-Buddhist culture.

During the Warring States period (16th century), the new military rulers again disdained Japan's cultural traditions, although they admired some aspects

Scroll depicting the evacuation of the Imperial family to Rokuhara. Hand scroll, color on paper. Kamakura period,

of dynastic art. Then, as Japan began to forge contacts with other countries besides China such as Borneo and some European nations, Japanese became exposed to completely different cultures.

These new influences encouraged the Japanese to cultivate freer, more candid artistic expression, greatly affecting the culture of the Azuchi-Momoyama Warring States era. The resulting body of art makes a strong impact, as if to exert enough energy to destroy the previous orders. The paintings done in the style of the Kano-ha and Rimpa schools of art are youthful and untamed in nature; exceeding even realistic art in expression, they seem to represent a return to a more primitive age. The art of the time featured bold designs with limited use of color but plenty of gold and silver. This art was intended to display the wide-ranging power of the ruling class. The

gorgeous opulence of many painted screens and Noh costumes of the Momoyama period testifies to the wealth of the time.

A new type of pattern was introduced at this time, taken from imported printed fabrics such as *Sarasa* (saraça), which was based upon an idealized form of just one plant, such as the ginger (*myoga*), cypress tree or lily; a pattern composed of a single plant was rarely seen in Japan before this. It was after the introduction of printed cloth that a single pine tree was first drawn on Noh costumes, and one chrysanthemum in a basket became a popular subject for paintings. The new military rulers, who opposed Chinese culture and favoured Noh and the tea ceremony, revolutionized Japanese military art, thereby supplanting the artistic ideas of their predecessors with their own.

Pink and White Japanese Plums. By Ogata Korin. Pair of four-folded screens.

14

PATTERNS IN THE EDO ERA

A new, revolutionary aesthetic emerged during the Edo period (1603–1867), which saw the development of three different cultures in Japan's three major cities: the modern military-dominated city of Edo, in the commercial Osaka, and Kyoto, where Imperial court culture still held sway.

In Edo, under samurai rule, strict control was imposed in order to create a stable social and political order, and ensuring obedience became more important than fostering new artistic trends. Compared to the somewhat mystical authority displayed by past rulers, the leaders of this period mainly were satisfied to confine their powers to the military realm. In 1617 the rulers built a gorgeous shrine to samurai culture, the Toshogu in Nikko. In screen paintings, artists of the Kano-ha and Rimpa schools pursued bold compositions of light and color and formalized their own styles. Later, urban artists replicated these styles in the *Ukiyo-e*, or woodblock prints. However, because of the intrusion of feudal power, and the strict regulations which governed everyday life, the people of Edo gradually lost their spirit of creativity.

In Osaka, on the other hand, the Edo period was a stable and prosperous age. Rather than the idle samurai of Edo, Osaka was dominated by prospering merchants who fostered a blossoming commercial era. Osaka's culture drew from its bustling street life, as well as influences from Kyoto, which is geographically close to Osaka.

Populated cities often encouraged the development of mass communication. During the Edo era, improvements in the technique of color woodblock print-making helped create a sophisticated mass media, including printed newspapers (*Kawaraban*); *Nishiki-e*, colored woodblock prints of actors and beautiful woman; and numerous written works. Beginning as illustrations for folding fans (*Ohgi-e*), which included simple printed patterns, a dyeing process called *Yuzen-zome* was developed and became very popular for fabric.

In the mid-17th century a book of clothing patterns called *Hiinagata* was published. However, the shogunate soon forbade common people from wearing flashy clothing, and various striped patterns became popular in place of natural motifs. Moreover, after family crests were worn on their costumes by leading actors, colorful and attractive crests became very fashionable, both for decorative use and as family symbols.

From the mid-18th century, the art of dwarf tree cultivation, or *Bonsai*, rapidly gained popularity. Those who appreciated Bonsai, from Daimyo to the common people, were not so interested in plants in their natural state. They preferred to create something artificial, something which had their own stamp on it. This novel form of art gave rise to numerous new types of plants and a preference for artificial rather than natural beauty become characteristic of the Edo period, perhaps arising from the predominance of urban culture. Crafts, too, were characterized by excessive processing and decoration, and they became more and more stylized.

In Kyoto, the elegant courtly spirit and lifestyles continued. In the mid-1600s, at approximately the

Edo period, 18th century. MOA Museum of Art, Shizuoka.

15

南見十二候

"Twelve Months in the South, The Seventh Month". Nishiki-e, Oban by Torii Kiyonaga. Edo period, 1784. The James

16

泰南見十二候

清長画

Michener Collection. The Honolulu Academy of Arts.

same time as the construction of the Toshogu Shrine in Nikko, Katsura Rikyu (the Katsura Imperial villa), and Shugakuin Rikyu (the Shugakuin Imperial villa), were built in Kyoto. Katsura Rikyu was planned by Hachijyo-miya as a villa for Prince Toshihito, who built Hachijyo's house with the support of the Shogun Hideyoshi Toyotomi, and Shugakuin Rikyu was planned by the Emperor Gomizuno-o. Both men were very talented in the tea ceremony, incense arts, flower arrangement, poetry and calligraphy, and their homes display a noble refinement; indeed, the homes can be regarded as the crystallization of the Japanese spirit. The use of space and the tranquility of Shugakuin Rikyu, for example, are completely different from the heavy feeling of the Toshogu Shrine— Shugakuin Rikyu reveals perfection in every little detail. In an era of diversified culture, the completely opposing aesthetics of the refinement of the traditional court and the opulence of the military class are perfectly expressed by the architecture of Katsura Rikyu and Shugakuin Rikyu versus that of the Toshogu Shrine.

The art of the Edo period is often thought to be overly decorative, weak and technically inferior. However, it could also be said that the popularization of culture was a very important trend. Art works from the previous era reveal an evolution of designs and patterns, but these designs were confined to the top social classes and were out of reach of the multitudes. Thus, the diffusion of designs and patterns through the merchant classes in Edo and Osaka during the Edo era meant greater overall change.

Japanese composition of figures and patterns is quite distinctive in its use of space. Unlike Persian carpets, for instance, where the pattern is composed to fill a specific space, the Japanese compose patterns to retain blank space. The work is considered a unity of picture and ornamentation, and the blank space is an important aspect of the whole. This idea of intentionally adding blank space is thought to be the influence of the Rimpa school, and it can also be observed in architecture such as that of Katsura Rikyu and Shugakuin Rikyu.

Patterns and designs originated from the need to fill the space. Japanese decoration distinguished itself by deliberately adding the blank space as a part of the composition.

APPENDIX: REGIONAL CHARACTERISTICS OF VEGETATION ANALYZED THROUGH FLOWER AND BIRD PATTERNS

Flower and bird patterns have long been popular in Japan. Usually common plants are chosen for motifs, but by examining the types of plants and birds which were selected for design motifs at various times, Japan's relationship with other countries and the feelings associated with various patterns becomes clear. The plants that were popular as the models for design patterns can be divided into three groups.

The first group contains the many plants of Japanese origin, such as cherry blossoms, camellias, maples and wisterias. Plants which grow in other parts of the world but have only been used as motifs for designs in Japan also belong to this first group. These include bush clovers, Chinese miscanthus and arrowroot. Plants that were imported as medicine and later used for design models, such as morning-glory and boneset, are also included. This grouping

reveals the Japanese fondness for that which is fragile and impermanent.

The second group contains plants of Chinese origin, and those plants that were originally used as design motifs in China, such as chrysanthemums, peonies, plums, pine trees, bamboo and peaches. While most of these subjects for design in China are useful household plants, the Chinese also assign symbolic meaning to them. For example, plums are edible fruits, and their flowers are respected as they blossom during the cold part of winter. Pine trees and bamboo are treasured as they are evergreens. They are not only used as construction materials but pine trees also provide resin and bamboo can be used as pulp. The combination of these respectable plants, *Shochikubai* (Pine-bamboo-plum), also came from China. Although in China this triad represents upstanding morals, in Japan it is used as a sign of good luck. These motifs were introduced to Japan with the introduction of Chinese prose and poetry, and along with their acceptance and fondness for Chinese cul-

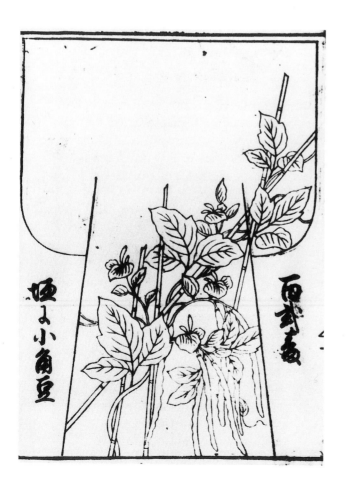

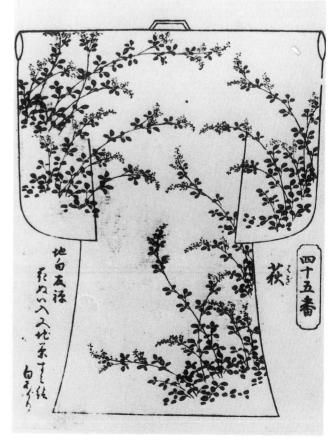

ture, the Japanese adopted these plant motifs as themes of patterns.

The third group includes plants that are of neither Japanese nor Chinese origin. Further subdividing by region, one set of plants originates in the early civilizations of Central Asia and Persia, and entered Japan through China and the Korean peninsula in ancient times. The vine motif, which was mentioned earlier, also came through this route. In early times, crops were normally transported as seedlings, but those originating in distant lands—such as melons, gourds, radishes, turnips and barley—were introduced as seeds. Although they do not seem foreign to Japanese as they were first brought to Japan long ago, the wild forms of these crops did not exist in China or Japan.

The second set of plants are those coming from Southeast Asia and Indian tropical regions. They were mainly brought into Japan through the China-Korea route, but some were introduced via the Ryukyu islands. Lotus, for example, which is associated with Buddism and originated in what is now Pakistan (Gandhara), was introduced to Japan via Central Asia and China. In China, the lotus is regarded as food as much as it is an ornamental garden plant, and when it first entered Japan, it was appreciated in much the same way. Imports from tropical Asia include the rice plant, an important grain in Japan, and ginger and taro, food crops which became popular design motifs.

Lastly, American culture was introduced by Europeans after the Azuchi-Momoyama period (1336–1598), and such foods as pumpkins came to Japan. The interesting shape of the pumpkin made it an appealing design theme.

Further comparison of the three regions of this last group indicates that West-Central Asia, with its dry climate and abundant pasturelands, supported livestock farming, while in the humid, forested lands of Southeast Asia, cultivation of crops was more popular. Thus, West Asia was the source of numerous, detailed patterns based on animals, but as a crop farming culture also existed in Japan, plant motifs from Southeast Asia were more realistically portrayed.

After the introduction of the cultures of various regions in early times came a period of national isolation, when typically Japanese patterns developed. Indeed, isolation was the key factor in the development of originality in Japanese patterns. With internationalization a growing trend in the future, patterns may become more diverse and complex—making it difficult to even identify source or nationality.

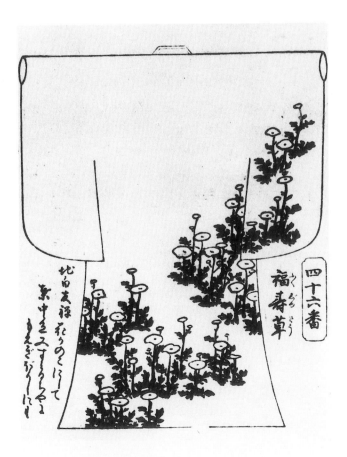

Hiinagata (The Pattern Book of Kosode)
From left to right:
Genroku Hiinagata of Flowers and Birds.
1703.

Genbun Hiinagata, "The *Otowa* Falls".
No. 45 *Hagi* (Japanes bush clover).
1737.

Genbun Hiinagata, "The *Otowa* Falls".
No. 46 *Fukuju-so* (Amur adonis).
1737.

From the Book of Japanese Art: "*Kosode*" Vol. 67, 1968
Published by the Shibundo Company, Tokyo.

PATTERNS AND THEIR MEANINGS

Reiko Morishige

1. KIKKO (Turtle's shell)

A representative pattern that means good luck

The common hexagonal pattern known as "Kikko" (turtle's shell) is a well-known symbol of good fortune in Japan. There are many such propitious symbols: In animals, they include the dragon, Chinese phoenix, crane and turtle, and among plants, the pine tree, bamboo, Japanese plum, chrysanthemum and peony. Chinese characters which can be seen on T-shirts purchased by visitors to Japan, such as 寿 (*kotobuki*) and 福 (*fuku*), are also signs of good luck. These symbols reflect common wishes for eternal youth, longevity, prosperity and wealth, among others.

The hexagonal Kikko pattern, called "beehive" in English and "turtle's shell" in Japanese, has an extremely long history. It first appeared in ancient civilizations of West Asia, as well as on colored earthenware in prehistoric Iran. The pattern was said to have been found on scraps of men's clothing in ninth century B.C. Assyria and in 12th century B.C. Babylon.

In parts of West Asia, particularly the Islamic countries, repetitive geometric shapes termed "arabesques" were popular. This suggests that the hexagonal shape of the Kikko may have originated in a purely geometric design, rather than the figurative forms of turtles' shells or beehives. However, its frequent usage indicates that the design carried deep meaning in many cultures.

The Kikko pattern was introduced to China through the Silk Road, which led from Persia and India to the desert towns of Western China, and although it was used as a decoration for woven materials and on the walls of temples, it was always seen as a symbol of power and spiritual strength. In China, a turtle has traditionally represented longevity, together with such imaginary animals as the dragon, Chinese phoenix and fire-breathing horse. It is believed that the patterns on a turtle's shell became associated with the hexagonal design during the height of the Silk Road, some 3,000 years ago.

The Kikko pattern came to Japan along with the introduction of Buddhism. It was first used to decorate materials and buildings, and in the Muromachi period (1336–1598); when Noh plays were popular, it was used as a popular design for stage decor and for the costumes worn by aristocratic characters and long-lived men. Today, the Kikko pattern can be found at Japanese wedding ceremonies. It appears on the bride's kimono and accessories, on the kimono of the wedding guests and even on the wallpaper of the wedding hall.

Man has forever wished for eternal youth, wealth and longevity. With the recent improvements in medicine and technology, the average life span in Japan has reached 80 years, and since World War II, the Japanese have achieved great prosperity, so what can Japanese people now wish for?

Long Overgarment: *Kikko-moyo Nuihaku Uchikake*. Momoyama period. Kodai-ji, Kyoto. "Uchikake" (a long overgarment) is a kind of formal dress for ladies of the samurai class. This overgarment was worn by the wife of Toyotomi Hideyoshi. Photograph provided by Kyoto National Museum.

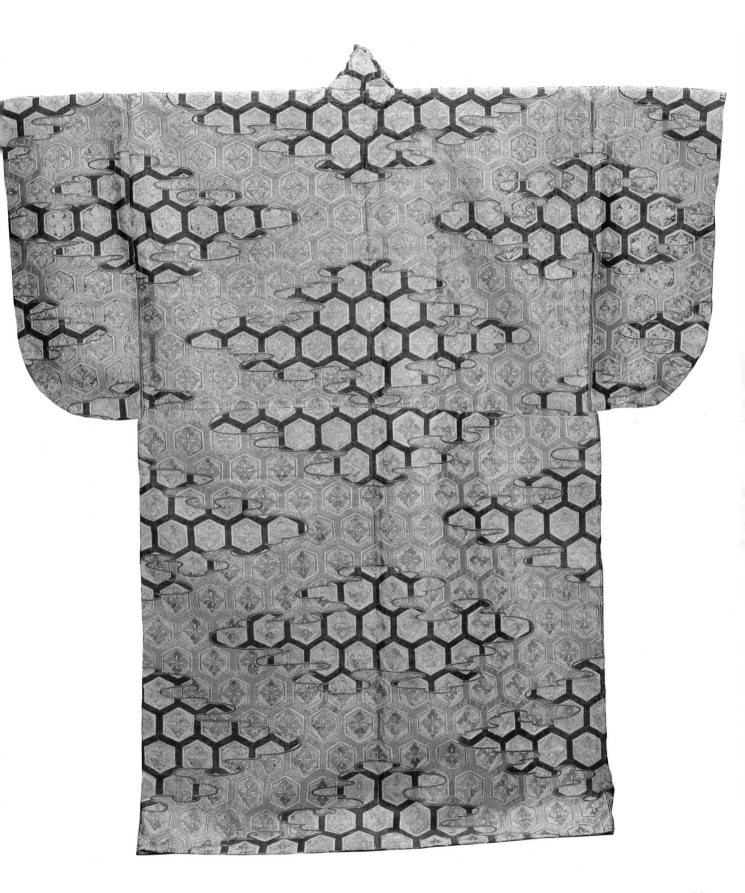

23

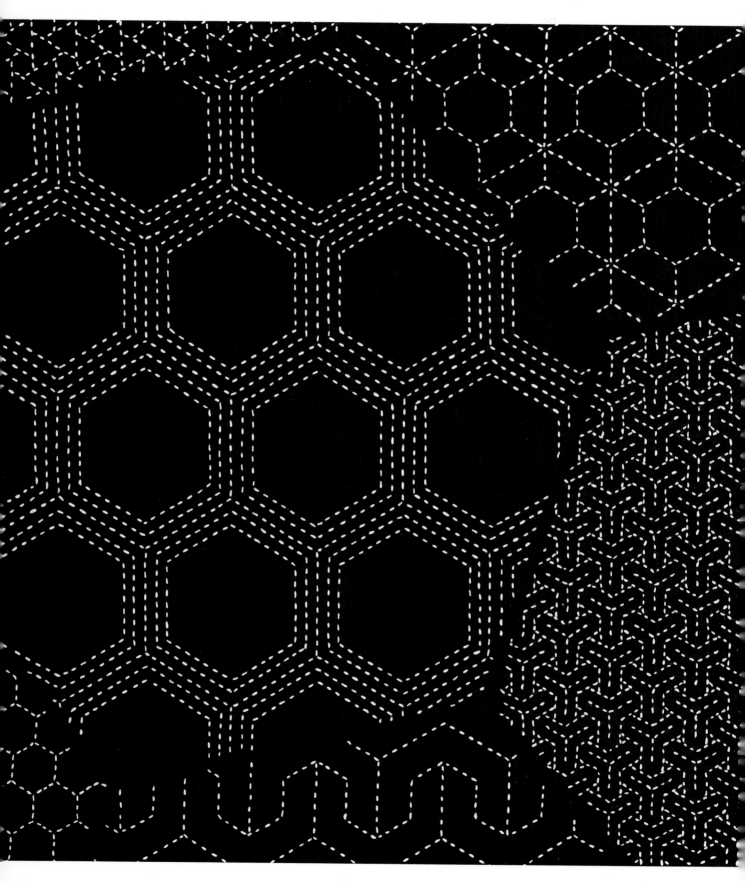

24

2. ASA-NO-HA (Hemp leaf)

A popular pattern in common use

Among the traditional patterns which have been most popular among Japanese over the years, one stands out: Asa-no-ha, or the hemp leaf pattern.

Even the common man with no interest in fabric design or patterns is sure to recognize this shape, although he may not know its name or history. If asked where he had seen it, he would probably find it difficult to respond clearly, conjecturing that "perhaps it was the pattern on the *kimono* someone was wearing" or "a pattern on the wooden box I had when I was small." This pattern has become so much a part of everyday life as usually to go unnoticed by Japanese.

There are two popular theories about the origin of this pattern. One school of thought insists that the Asa-no-ha is purely Japanese; the other claims that it was introduced to Japan from India via China. While neither theory can be confirmed, it's clear that the Asa-no-ha pattern began to figure in Japanese art during the Heian period (794–1192 A.D). It was then found on fabric used to clothe images of Buddha and in Buddhist paintings; later it was incorporated into building decor.

To some Japanese craftsmen, the Asa-no-ha's repeating pattern of spokes radiating from a central white hub presents an impression of light and the radiating power of Buddha. Whether used alone or repeated, however, this is a very useful pattern for those involved in design, as it can be used in varying sizes and with spaces of nearly any size.

Although the Asa-no-ha pattern was originally associated with religious applications, it gained wide acceptance among common people in the Edo period, when the influence of popular—rather than aristocratic—culture reached its zenith. Kabuki theater, which began during this period, became wildly popular, and it greatly influenced many aspects of people's lives. The clothes and the hair styles of Kabuki actors were regarded as the latest in trend-setting fashions. The Asa-no-ha pattern is said to have become popular after it was used on an actor's stage costume, but its appeal was no doubt strengthened through the spread of *Nishiki-e,* color woodblock prints of popular actors.

The art form of *Ukiyo-e* (woodblock prints) also attested to the popularity of Asa-no-ha patterns during the Edo era. Famed Ukiyo-e artists such as Utamaro have portrayed young girls and geisha as well as men wearing kimono and *obi* adorned with Asa-no-ha designs. As dyeing techniques became perfected, the Asa-no-ha pattern became a more frequent sight on kimono fabric and other everyday goods. And while the origins of the name Asa-no-ha are unclear, it's certain that this pattern was already called by that name during the Edo period.

Hemp has been cultivated since ancient times. Before the Muromachi period when cotton was first imported and its later popularization in the Edo period, hemp was the most common raw material for making clothes. The Asa-no-ha gained its name for its resemblance to the leaf of the hemp plant.

As hemp is a strong, fast-growing plant, the Asa-no-ha pattern was traditionally favored for babies' diapers and bedclothes to reflect the hope that one's baby would grow as strong as hemp. The Asa-no-ha pattern was also a favorite for "Sashiko" work, since the pattern looked most attractive when displayed on cotton dyed in indigo and sewn in layers.

Classical Puppet Theater: *Awa Jyoruri Ningyo.* Awa Juro Yashiki, Tokushima. "Ningyo Jyoruri" is a form of classical puppet theater in which the dolls (*ningyo*) are manipulated while the narrator recites the story (*jyoruri*) to the accompaniment of the *samisen.* This costume is for Osome, the young heroine in one of the most popular plays. Photograph provided by Asahi Shimbun Publishing Company.

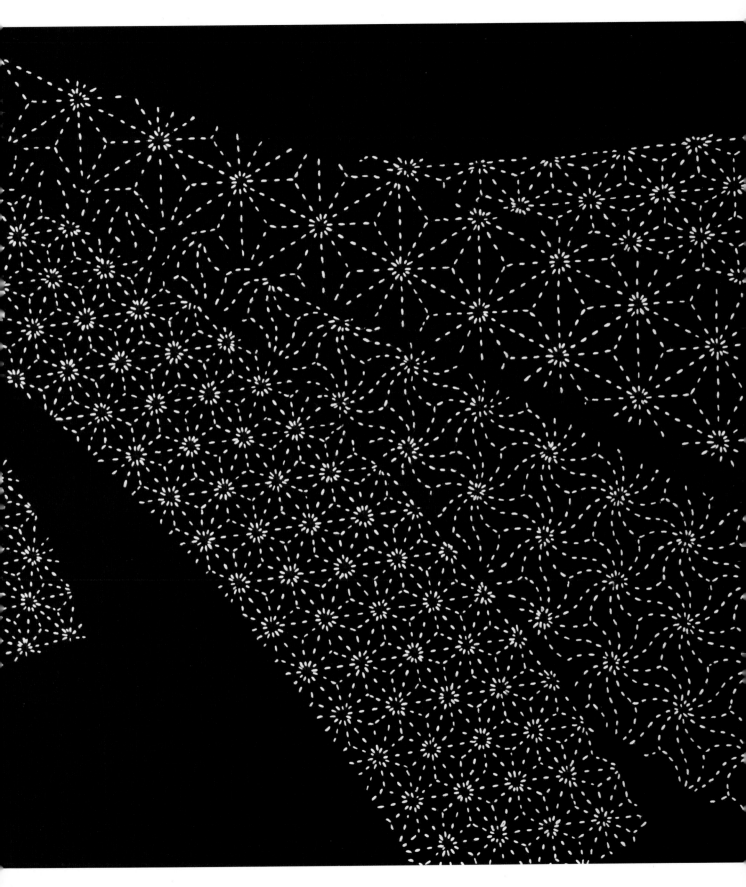

3. HISHI (Diamond shape)
A geometric, diamond shape frequently seen in Japanese homes

The Hishi or diamond pattern is clearly of geometric origin. As it is a basic form like the circle and triangle, it probably existed in various parts of the world from ancient times.

A distinctive Hishi pattern forms the background design on woven silk material that dates from earliest times. A pattern which is formed by repeating a geometric shape is usually called *Waritsuke moyo* (sequential pattern). Circles, Kikko (turtle's shell) and Hishi patterns are typical Waritsuke patterns, and were originally used as basic decorative patterns on fabrics. The popularity of the Hishi pattern stems from its utility in ordering a composition, even one containing figurative forms.

In the Nara period (600–784 A.D.), sophisticated techniques of textile manufacture already existed, and this technology, which had been practiced only by aristocrats, spread to the common people by the beginning of the Edo period. During the Muromachi and Momoyama periods when trade flourished, technical specialists brought their luxurious fabrics with them from China and settled in Kyoto, the center of culture. At the time, the aristocratic form of Noh was very popular, and Noh actors playing the main roles spent lavishly on the lush fabrics used to make their costumes. This encouraged the textile manufacturers of Kyoto to be extremely creative and meticulous, a tradition that continues today. They developed a variety of Hishi patterns as a decorative element for their fabrics.

No one knows when this pattern was first called Hishi, the name of a water chestnut which grows in ponds and swamps. The stem of the Hishi reaches the water surface, then it sends forth innumerable leaves which are of irregular, elongated diamond shape.

In contrast to the Hishi patterns found on ornate silk materials, other types of Hishi patterns exist. Developing from their everyday use by common people, these textile forms still have considerable popularity. One of them was first employed in an embroidery style called *Kogin*, which developed in the Tohoku area, in the north of Japan. In Kogin, Hishi patterns are sewn with white cotton thread onto linen, which is first dyed in indigo.

In the Edo period, cotton was an article of value. Little was imported from abroad, and common people were prohibited from using it. Thus in order to strengthen the linen that was commonly used to make warmer clothing, pieces of linen were sewn on top of each other. The Hishi pattern was favored as a design which could be created by simple stitching. There are various other Hishi patterns which were born from women's need to create beautiful and comfortable clothes with a limited supply of materials. These designs are still loved by women who like to create their own clothing.

The Hishi pattern has also been used as a single design, rather than repeated in the background, on the ornate crests used throughout Japanese history as symbols for samurai and noble clans. During the Kamakura period and the Warring States period (1192–1333), warriors' flags featured the crests of their patrons. However, in the Edo period, the crests appeared as small designs in specified places on kimono and other clothing. Inevitably, the crest designs themselves came to be surrounded by repeating circles or squares, and the Hishi pattern, which is a modified square, became valued as a basic design.

Later in the Edo era, when the general public was permitted to adopt family crests, each family developed its own symbol. Merchants used them on the signs of their shops or on the paper used to wrap packages. The tradition of family crests remains with us: Even today, a formal kimono bears a crest, stores feature crests on their signs, and they can be seen on the company badges worn by employees of large firms. Most of the major Japanese trading firms, which have branches all over the world, have as their corporate symbols designs which originated as family crests.

Noh Outer Robe Nuihaku:
Iroe Tsuruhishi-mon Karaori.
Edo period. Ishikawa Prefectural
Museum of Art.
"Karaori" (Chinese weave)
is a kind of silk fabric which
was worn by court nobles
or Noh actors.
Crane and diamond-shape
embroidered designs.

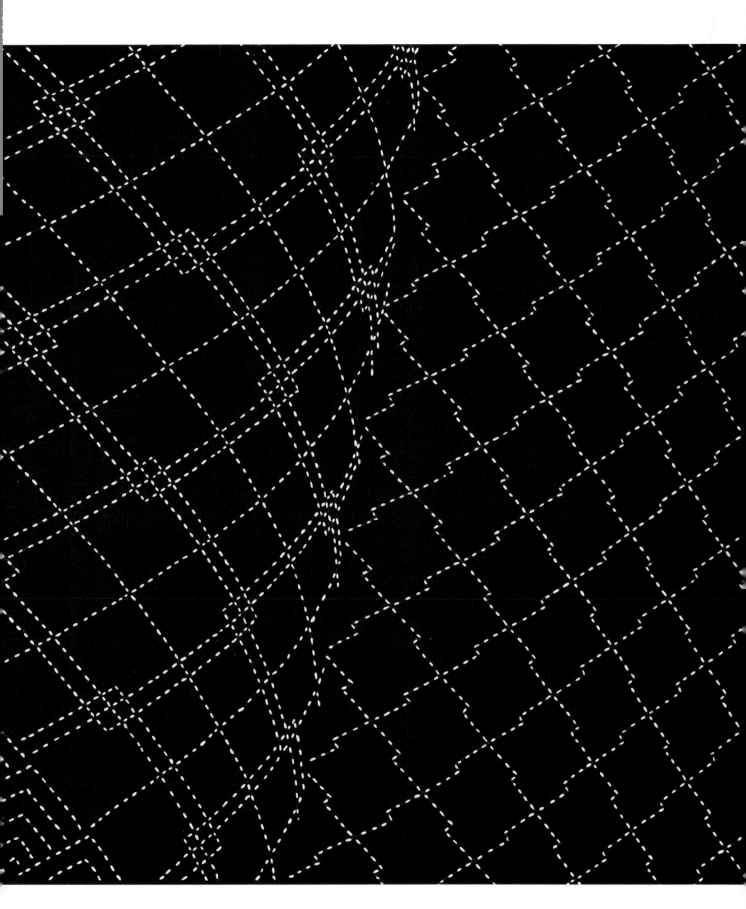

4. RYUSUI & NAMI (Running water and waves)
Diverse design forms that display a Japanese sensibility

Water has been the cradle of culture in many parts of the world. As is clear from local myths and religious ceremonies, water has not only been a daily necessity throughout history, but it has also been embued with spiritual meaning and mysterious powers. However, there is little to indicate that water was particularly important as a design motif. Among the Egyptian art that was created near the Nile River, works featuring water or sea-like patterns are rare. Running water and wave patterns can be found in China, however, and China's various design motifs greatly influenced Japanese arts. Though the usage of these patterns is less diverse in China than in Japan, they usually appear with the figures of dragons on such objects as chinaware and lacquerware. It could be said that running water and wave patterns are among the most sophisticated and developed motifs to be found in Japan.

Living on islands surrounded by water, practicing fishing and farming, Japanese have a special feeling for the sea. They regard the ocean and water with a combination of familiarity and awe, leading them to pay particular attention to other water forms such as clouds, rain, fog, mist and dew. A famous essay from the Kamakura period (*Hojoki*, 1212) which begins: "The flow of a river is eternal and its waters are never the same," reveals the Japanese tendency to portray life and emotions by alluding to water, nature and the passage of time. This well-known statement has been echoed since by the themes of many popular Japanese literary works. In fact, water and waves were often chosen as motifs after their appearance in the Manyoshu, the oldest collection of Japanese poetry. The poems in the Manyoshu depict in very sensitive fashion the water dripping from thawing snow, rough surging seas, ripples in a small pond and the slow flow of great rivers.

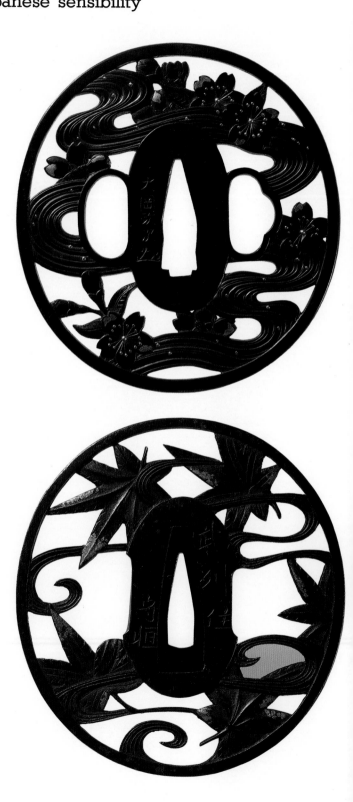

Top: *Tsuba* Sword Guard, cherry blossoms in stream design, copper. Edo period, 17th century. The Tokugawa Art Museum, Aichi. Bottom: *Tsuba* Sword Guard, stream and maple cutout design, iron. Edo period, 18th century. The Tokugawa Art Museum, Aichi.

Running water and wave patterns in Heian period art (794–1192A.D.) were already drawn with softly curved lines, revealing Japanese tastes. As literature and art arose that were uniquely Japanese (rather than adaptations of Chinese art), literature and art such as the Japanese syllabary *(Kana)*, 31-syllable poems (*Waka*) and *Yamato-e* paintings included the softly curved lines expressing running water and wave patterns that were favored by the aristocrats of the time. When their popularity was at its height, these motifs were used to decorate kimono, Noh costumes and chinaware. Wave patterns, basically composed of curved lines, add movement to a design, and they are effective as a motif to divide space or change scenes, as can be seen with *Kasumi* (mist) patterns.

Water and wave patterns showed dramatic change during the late Momoyama (1573–1598) and Edo periods. It was at this time when popular culture became increasingly sophisticated, as wealthy merchants began to patronize the arts. Compared to the samurai class, the merchants were of lower social status, but they were wealthier and often displayed better taste than the samurai.

Artists of the Koetsu and Rimpa schools of art were extremely active at this time, creating ornamental, highly decorative art and craft works.

Running water and wave patterns became important motifs in these works, and they were joined by figures of birds, fish, flowers and scenic motifs, and at times, with rabbits. In any combination, it is apparent that the artists harnessed considerable passion and energy in their depictions of water and waves.

Among the wave patterns is a unique design called Seikai-ha, which developed from different roots than the others. Unlike the other designs composed of discrete curves, the Seika-ha is made up of overlapping curves. It first appears in the ancient pottery wares of the Sasan Age in Persia. In Japan it has been found on the clothing worn by Haniwa, the clay figures of the Tumulus period of Japan. It later appears on Chinese and Japanese ceramics and also on woven fabrics.

Highly abstract in appearance and freely patterned, water and waves remain stimulating artistic motifs today.

Comb: *Miho-no-matsubara Maki-e Kushi.* Edo period. Suntory Museum of Art, Tokyo. A woman's comb bearing the name of "*Miho-no-matsubara*," an are in Shizuoka Prefecture famous for its beautiful pine-dotted beach.

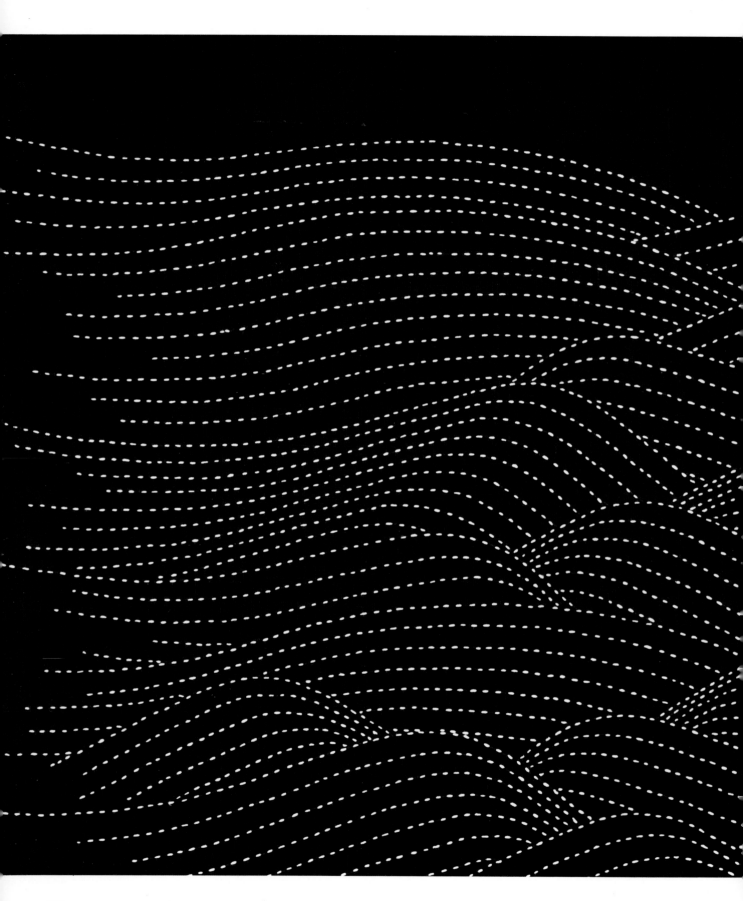

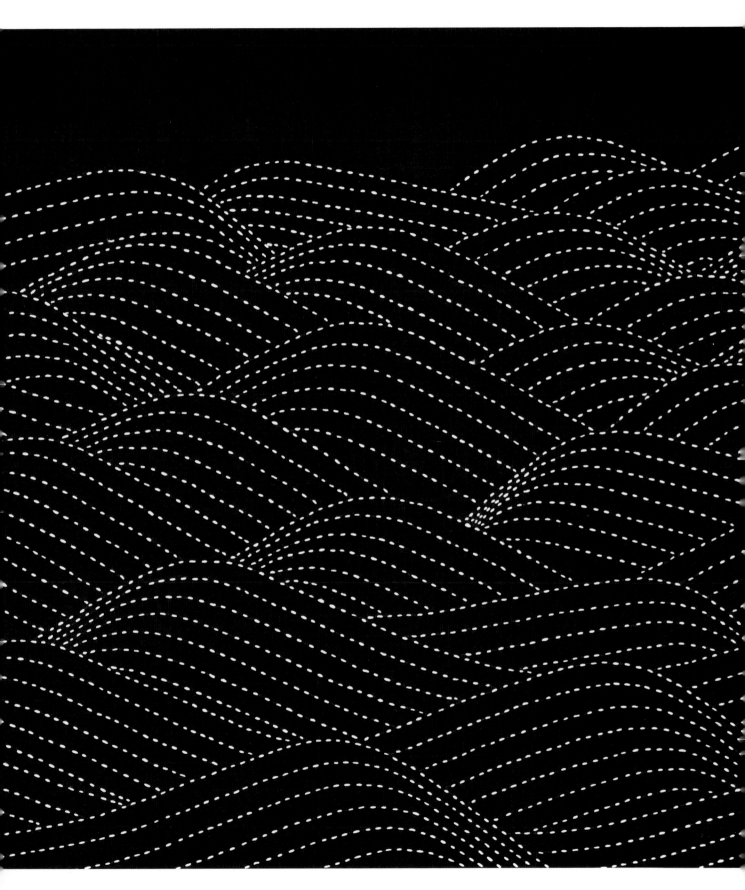

5. AMI, KUMI, MUSUBI (Meshwork, braids, plaits)
Designs developed from practical applications

I did not know how to respond when, attending a friend's party in New York a few years ago, an American woman approached me and inquired: "Is your house made of wood, clay and paper?" She was a great fan of old Japanese movies and evidently had acquired her knowledge of Japan through watching these obscure films, which I know only by name. Certainly, seen on film, Japanese houses did look as though they were made only of wood, clay and paper, as wood was used for the framework and interior decor, and other common materials included bamboo, clay walls, roofs of straw, tiles, tatami made of rush and paper screens.

Among these traditional materials, bamboo, bark and straw were always considered most important, after wood. They were usually bundled or braided. Of course, knitting or braiding these flexible materials was practiced all over the world, since these techniques developed from such basic hand movements as folding, bending and knotting, but knitting and plaiting were especially popular in Japan, and as natural materials were plentiful, they were used for a host of everyday necessities. After these techniques began to be applied to architectural works, the search for new housing materials led to the development of a variety of patterns with diverse uses. With the growing sophistication in housing design and the popularization of the tea ceremony, these patterns became more and more decorative. Even the fences around a house combined various building materials and gave rise to many different decorative forms. Each form was given a name and remains popular today.

The technique of plaiting cords, on the other hand, originally came to Japan from China. It was refined, and a typical Japanese style was established. Cords were traditionally used as decoration on Buddhist altars, on the formal kimono worn by aristocrats and on furniture. In fact, study of antique Japanese armor and escutcheons reveals a surprising variety in the styles of plaited cords.

The many different ways of plaiting cords which developed varied according to their purpose. In the Heian period, well-bred young women studied cord plaiting, along with Waka (31-syllable poetry), music and painting. Later, plaiting became an important element of tea ceremonies, and the established techniques of plaiting became a part of the everyday lives of common people.

Meshwork, braiding and plaiting were first developed as decorative skills. However, these beautiful forms were later adopted as patterns adorning craft works and dyed prints. In the Momoyama period, bold designs were especially favored for *Kosode* (a short-sleeved silk garment—the old name for kimono) and on Noh theater costumes. They became very popular because, when used as a basic pattern, knitted and braided designs worked well with every motif. The knotted cord pattern became a favorite for somewhat bold designs.

Today I live in a house made of concrete, iron, glass and wood. Much as I would like to live in a house made of natural materials, carefully constructed by hand, it is difficult to procure these natural materials today, and there are few skilled workers who can build traditional homes. Sadly, to live in a house made of natural materials is a costly dream that can rarely be realized today.

A Long-sleeved Silk Garment (*Furisode*): *Monchirimen-ji Noshi Yuzenzome Furisode*. Edo period. Society of Yuzenzome. "Yuzenzome" is a method of dyeing which produces brilliant, decorative textiles. This kimono is especially famous for its boldness and splendor. Photograph provided by Kyoto National Museum.

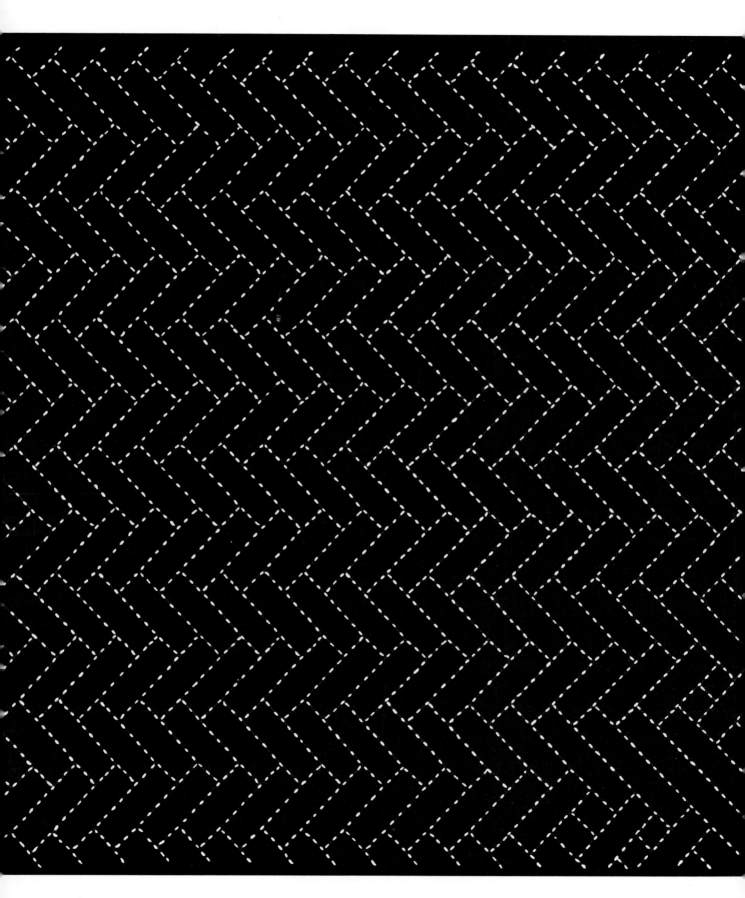

6. SHIMA & KOSHI (Stripes and checks)

Can be either sophisticated or simple. In Japanese: *iki* and *yabo*

In the Meiji period, a new, more refined type of Kabuki play was created for the common people. As depicted in *Nishiki-e* color prints, one can see that a surprising number of the Kabuki costumes of that period are adorned with stripes. In one Nishiki-e print, every figure is wearing a striped costume. Samurai warriors, young merchants and students all wear different kinds of stripes, and girls and mothers sport striped *Haori* (a short coat) and striped obi, each of a style expressing youthfulness, boldness or poverty. There are three types of striped patterns: *Tate-jima* (vertical stripes), *Yoko-jima* (horizontal stripes) and *Koshi* (checks). Checks are said to have been developed from stripes.

How did stripes come to be so popular, among commoners as well as on stage? The first woven clothes were probably solid colors, using plants that were easily available. But when several natural materials were woven together, striped patterns naturally resulted. Thus, stripes are throught to have existed from ancient times. Among Japanese historical remains, however, striped motifs are rare.

Although stripes are mentioned in the Manyoshu, the oldest collection of Japanese poetry, no actual striped material from that period has been found, not even in the collection of the Shosoin in Nara, which is a treasure trove of historical remains. The items in the Shōsōin Repository are mainly the belongings of aristocrats. As striped fabrics were mainly worn by common people, they were disdained by aristocrats. According to writings on ancient court costumes, striped apparel was considered too casual, and was forbidden in the Imperial Court. Its use was relegated to lower officials, retainers and children.

In the Muromachi and the Momoyama periods, the formerly unpopular striped fabric began attracting popular attention. Beautiful striped silk woven fabrics came into Japan through trade with China, and colorful cotton prints and striped clothing from India, Java, Thailand and Indonesia were imported by the Portuguese, the Spanish and the Dutch. Stripes came to be considered an extravagant and novel design, favored by the trend-setting tea ceremony masters as an exotic touch. They were also introduced for Noh costumes.

During the flourishing merchant culture of the Edo period, wealthy upper class merchants spent lavishly on clothing and other luxuries. However, as the sums they spent on decorative objects increased, the quality and beauty of the works themselves declined, resulting in a flood of vulgar, imitative goods. Sensible people began to express their dislike of vulgarity and conspicuous consumption, finally forcing the feudal government to enforce a ban against extravagance. As a result, the fashion-conscious began to seek sophistication through simple designs, and stripes gained a smart image. With a promotional boost from being used on Kabuki costumes, stripes became extremely popular. Most fashionable was striped clothing bearing the name of a leading Kabuki actor. People began to note the subtle differences in stripes, such as irregularity and color hues; they began to differentiate between bold and restrained stripes, smart stripes and unrefined ones. The popularization of cotton coincided with this trend. As indigo was the dye most commonly used at the time, the durability and beauty of indigo was widely put to advantage with striped patterns.

Contemporary Japanese society, with its emphasis on material affluence to enhance one's everyday life, is often compared to the prosperous culture of Edo. Today's Japanese society is said to value expensive and showy goods, no matter whether in good or bad taste. However, young, talented fashion designers are now beginning to reconsider the beauty of stripes. In the past, vertical stripes were thought to be smart as they set off the shape of kimono. Today, however, horizontal stripes are more popular as their image is original and sporty.

Hosoban Nishiki-e, by Katsukawa Shunei: *Tsumoru Koi Yuki no Seki-no-To*, modeled by Kabuki star Ishikawa Monnosuke Kambe, II. Edo period. Tobacco and Salt Museum, Tokyo. This Nishiki-e print depicts a Kabuki star popular with the common people in the Edo period.

7. KASUMI (Haze/mist)
Motifs found in Japanese literature and paintings

When on a journey you come across a scene often depicted in traditional Japanese paintings, such as the mountains disappearing and reappearing in the mist after the rain has fallen, you can't help but react with pleasure. For the Japanese, fog or mist trailing over mountains and fields is a familiar and agreeable sight. Since Japan is a grouping of several mountainous islands, with abundant greenery and a generally humid climate, the people often experience various types of fog, mist and haze, according to weather conditions and temperature. Natural veils of fog shrouding mountain tops and blanketing fields on spring mornings or autumn eves were the subjects of numerous literary works from olden days. In many Japanese paintings, mist is effectively used to create space, in a form of expression quite different from the realistic Western artistic perspective.

Kasumi (mist), as used for visual expression, can be roughly classified into two types. One is used for shading, to express depth in landscape paintings. This technique is commonly seen in *Suibokuga* (sumi paintings), first introduced from China in the Muromachi period, as well as in more realistic, modern Japanese paintings. The other type is the formalized Kasumi pattern which appears in *Emaki-mono* (picture scrolls). The latter became popular as a design for handicrafts, on dyed materials and on woven fabric. We will focus on the latter Kasumi pattern.

The Tale of Genji, Japan's oldest full-length novel, was written in the middle of the Heian period (the early 11th century). Later, a picture scroll of The Tale of Genji appeared, in which the story was written and illustrated on a long horizontal scroll, as were many tales at that time. The illustrations were typically drawn from a bird's-eye perspective; many were quite bold in composition. By painting part of a scroll scene in the shape of a cloud and using curved lines as dividers, the Kasumi pattern could be very effective in indicating a change in plot or in implying the passage of time.

Later, in Japanese paintings depicting battles (*Senki*) or "genre pictures" (*Fuzoku-ga*), Kasumi patterns were used to convey the coexistence of opposing elements, such as high-class and low-class people, war and peace, dream and reality and past and present. Thus, the Kasumi pattern had a fixed symbolic meaning for the Japanese. Moreover, in craft works and on dyed fabrics, the Kasumi pattern was used as an element for arranging a composition, in order to link together the various elements in the art work.

In brief, the Kasumi pattern was used effectively to express change in a painted scene or to break up the space. Helped by the viewer's imagination, Kasumi deletes that which is unnecessary, and hints at the picture's unseen elements. In this respect, the Kasumi pattern may have much in common with the Japanese way of thinking. It is often said that the Japanese tend to give unclear explanations and speak in an ambiguous way. Be it a good or a bad thing, the vagueness of Japanese language and its way of expression is undeniable. Suggesting rather than affirming, while allowing vagueness and clarity to coexist, perhaps reveals the Kasumi present in the Japanese mind.

Landscape Musashino Area: *Musashino-zu Byobu*.
Pair of six-fold screens, paper.
Edo period, 17th century. Tokyo National Museum.

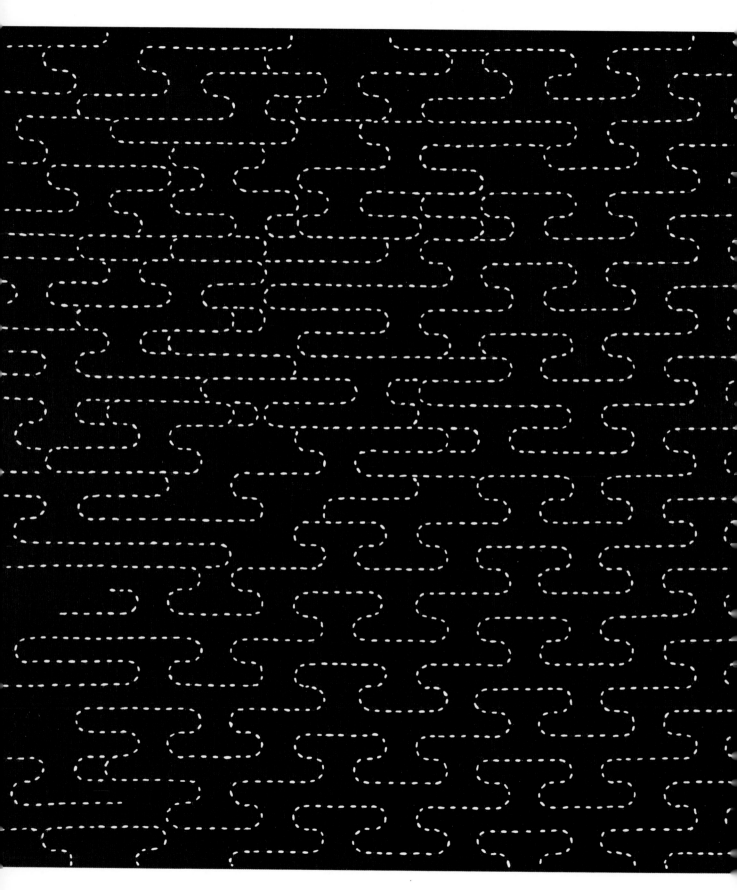

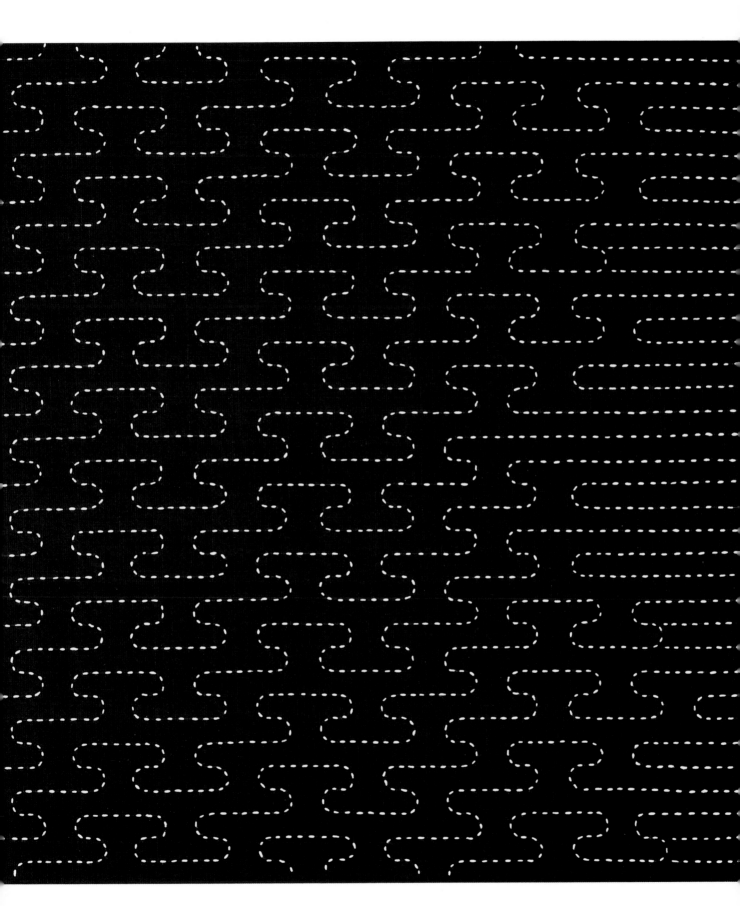

8. UROKO & SANKAKU (Fish scales and triangles)

Patterns with a strong impact

A geometric pattern made up of repeating triangles makes a strong statement when it appears on Noh-theater costumes.

A tragic and terrifying story of spurned love called "Musume-dojo-ji" has long been a popular subject for Noh plays, Kabuki and Japanese dances. The story goes like this: A young woman falls in love with a traveling monk and waits for his return. However, the monk does not show on the day he has promised to return. In turns grieving and furious at his treachery, the half-crazed woman, hair disheveled and eyes aglow, chases the errant monk. As she runs, she transforms herself into a snake, and slithers across the river heading for the temple to which the monk escaped. By the time she arrives, the monk has already hid himself in a temple bell, so the spiteful snake winds herself around the bell, burning the bell, the monk and herself in flames of hatred and betrayal.

In plays, the Uroko (fish scale) pattern adorns the woman's costume which is revealed when she flings off her beautiful human dress and transforms herself into a snake. The pattern is typically drawn in gold or silver on a white fabric, but some patterns are applied to red or black material. Under the stage lights, the sparkling Uroko design strengthens the impact of the terrible transformation.

In Noh plays, costumes with Uroko patterns are always used to represent the transformation of beautiful women into dreadful, jealous characters, consumed by revenge. The patterns can be seen on the kimono of a demon assuming the form of a noble lady to seduce a samurai warrior, or a dead mother who retains a strong attraction to this world even after her death.

The triangle pattern was originally called the *Kyoshi-mon* (saw-tooth pattern), and it has been popular in many parts of the world throughout history. It was most likely introduced to Japan from China, and was first used as a design on earthenware and on bronze swords during the Yayoi period (600 A.D.). The Kyoshi pattern also appeared on Haniwa clay images and on the walls of decorated tombs. For the Yayoi people, the pattern formed by repeated triangles was apparently a symbol of illness, but at the same time, it was believed to be a talisman against evil. Even in China, this pattern has been used as a charm since ancient times, and it was thought to symbolize rebirth and revival. Thus the pattern was often used on the walls of tombs and at gravesites, with the aim of driving away evil spirits and hastening the rebirth of the dead.

Although it's not known when the Kyoshi pattern came to be called the Uroko or scale pattern, the pattern has always been thought to symbolize snake scales, not fish scales. The three-scale pattern often seen on family crests today is said to have originated from the designs on the clan banners carried by samurai warriors. It is believed that they were inspired to use it by the oft-told tale of a samurai in the Kamakura period who, when praying for his family's prosperity at a shrine, spied a giant snake which left behind three-scale fragments.

The Uroko pattern is still popular in craft works, on dyed fabrics and on woven materials, owing to the simplicity and clarity of its design. Although its shape is simple, the pattern is still beloved as it enables the craftsman to realize a great variety of forms, depending on the arrangement, composition and colors selected.

Noh Stage of *Aoi-no-Ue*. "Aoi-no-Ue" is a story in Genji Monogatari (The Tale of Genji), famous for its depiction of a noble lady in anguish from jealousy. Under the Noh stage lights, the sparkling Uroko pattern strengthens the impact of the terror transformation. Photograph by Shozo Masuda.

53

9. TOMOE & MANJI (Whirls and reverse swastika)
Designs that project energy

The origin of the Tomoe pattern is not known, but as a spiritual image and as an expression of perpetual energy, the Tomoe (whirl) pattern was common to various parts of the world thousands of years ago. Ancient man's act of transforming a curve into a circle, then into a scroll, seems to be a natural result of the instinctive human need for self-expression. As for its shape, it has been described in many ways: as the image of a snake, a whirlpool, an embryo, or as a symbol of universal energy. In Japan, the Magatama (a comma-shaped bead) is an ancient accessory in the Tomoe shape, while the Tomoe pattern found on drums from the Heian period is thought to be the oldest example of this design. In the Kamakura period, it was widely used on family crests, arms and accessories.

The Manji pattern, which is probably an expanded form of the Tomoe pattern, is said to have originated as a character of Sanskrit, the language used in ancient India. Some scholars describe it as a symbol of movement; they claim that a pattern including both clockwise and counter-clockwise shapes arose from the theory of cosmic movement or the movement of the sun. During the fifth century B.C. in India, a clockwise Manji pattern was used as a symbol of the sun. Since then, the pattern has been drawn in red to symbolize its power to bring about glory and prosperity. It was introduced to Japan from China along with Buddhism. A Manji pattern on the breast of an image of Buddha denotes his goodness, and it implies that his mercy and grace are as vast as the ocean and as abundant as the clouds.

The Manji pattern itself is now treated more like a mark than a pattern in Japan, with the figure often used on maps to indicate the location of temples.

Noh Outer Robe (*Atsuita*): *Moegi, Benidan-Koshi, Hiun, Manji-mon Atsuita.*
Edo period, 17th century. The Tokugawa Art Museum, Aichi
Brocade squares of "flying" clouds and reverse swastikas on green or fan twill-weave background, silk.

Another pattern, Sayagata (the Saya pattern), is formed through repetition of the Manji image. Saya is also a name for glossy woven silk fabric, which was imported mainly in the period between the Momoyama and Edo eras, and was often used for opulent kimono. As the repeated Manji pattern was a popular background motif on this fabric, the pattern was named Sayagata. It remains popular today.

Today, men tend to pay too much attention to artificial energy forms such as atomic energy, forgetting the natural energy from the universe that keeps us alive. If men would renew their respect for the positive energy forces in the universe, they would be less likely to harness energy through nuclear weapons and other destructive means.

Noh Long Over-Jacket (*Kariginu*): *Zuiun Tomoe-mon*. Edo period. The Tokugawa Art Museum, Aichi. "Kariginu" is a silk garment for Noh actors. This pattern was used for the costumes of noble people.

10. SHO CHIKU BAI (Pine tree-bamboo-Japanese plum)
The "Three Friends"—signifies happiness and good fortune

The Sho (pine tree), Chiku (bamboo) and Bai (Japanese plum) are popular plant patterns which symbolize happiness. When the three are combined together, they form a pattern called Kissho (good fortune). There are many combinations of plants, or plants with animals, which have symbolic meaning in China, but the Sho-Chiku-Bai pattern was so suited to Japanese tastes that it was rapidly adopted by Japanese. This threefold pattern reflects the Chinese belief that odd numbers are lucky. Odd numbers are often used to count important people or things, such as "The Three Sages" and "The Seven Wise Men." Three and seven are still considered to be the luckiest among all numbers.

According to an ancient Japanese belief, the spirits dwell in huge trees, and the trees are used by God to descend to earth. Thus, massive trees have special spiritual significance in the precincts of shrines and temples, with some having a longer history than the Shinto shrines they shade.

While pine trees are not thought to soar to the sky to ease God's descent, as cedars and other tall trees supposedly do, they are favored as special trees for their ability to keep their needles all winter long and for their strength in taking root on overhanging cliffs and enduring wind and waves. They are also respected for their pleasing forms, which grow more beautiful as the trees age.   Huge pine trees which

Covered Box, pine and Japanese apricot stylized shore design, *maki-e* lacquer, on wood. Muromachi period

are found in shrine precincts and on the grounds of noblemens' estates are seen as symbols of longevity and authority. They are also used for decoration. Noh plays were once performed in the open air before a large pine tree, and old pine trees are still painted on the wall of Noh theater stages and are also often seen on the Kabuki stage.

Bamboo is very familiar to the Japanese, both for its ornamental value and as a source of countless items for practical use. It is used in Shinto ceremonies as a symbol of vitality, liveliness and prosperity, as it grows exceedingly fast and straight. Moreover, the rustling leaves of the bamboo impart a lonely feeling, and its insubstantial, swaying form suggests uncertainly or the Buddhist idea of the transience of life. Bamboo is an important element of Japanese aesthetics, and it often appears in literary works depicting the Japanese sense of beauty.

Takarabune, Enamelled ware.
By Nonomura Ninsei.
Edo period, 17th century.
Fujita Art Museum, Osaka.
The works of Ninsei, a well-known ceramicist of Kyoyaki ware, are characterized by a beautiful combination of colors.

The popular Japanese plum motif also originated in China. Artists of the Rimpa School in the Edo period filled their works with the beloved Japanese plum, a tree whose flowers are not as showy as the peony or cherry tree blossoms, but which blooms during the coldest part of the winter. Many art works using the Japanese plum as a motif were created in the Edo period, and they have exerted a great influence on present craft works.

The combined Sho-Chiku-Bai pattern is a more realistic image than many other, abstract Japanese patterns. In this pictorial motif, the original shapes of the three plants are clearly drawn. The pattern is still widely used, especially as a New Year decoration.

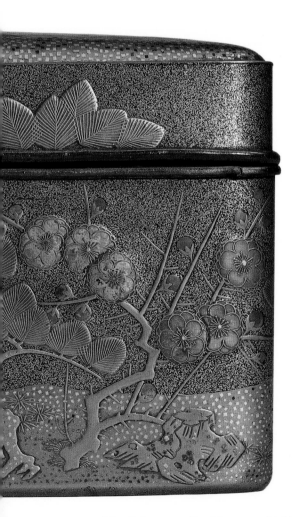

15—16th century. The Tokugawa Art Museum, Aichi.

59

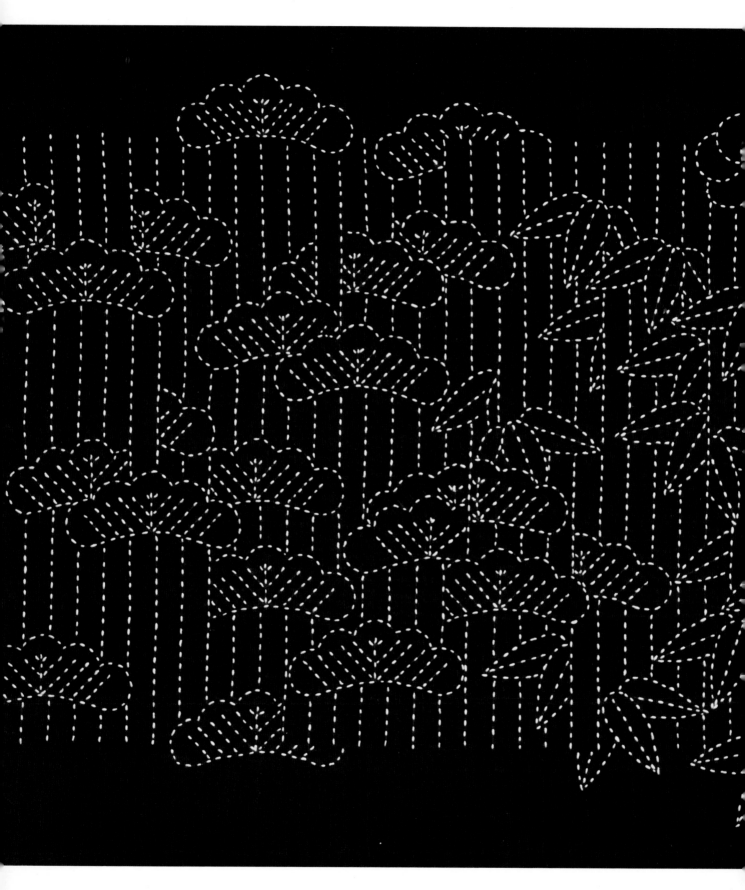

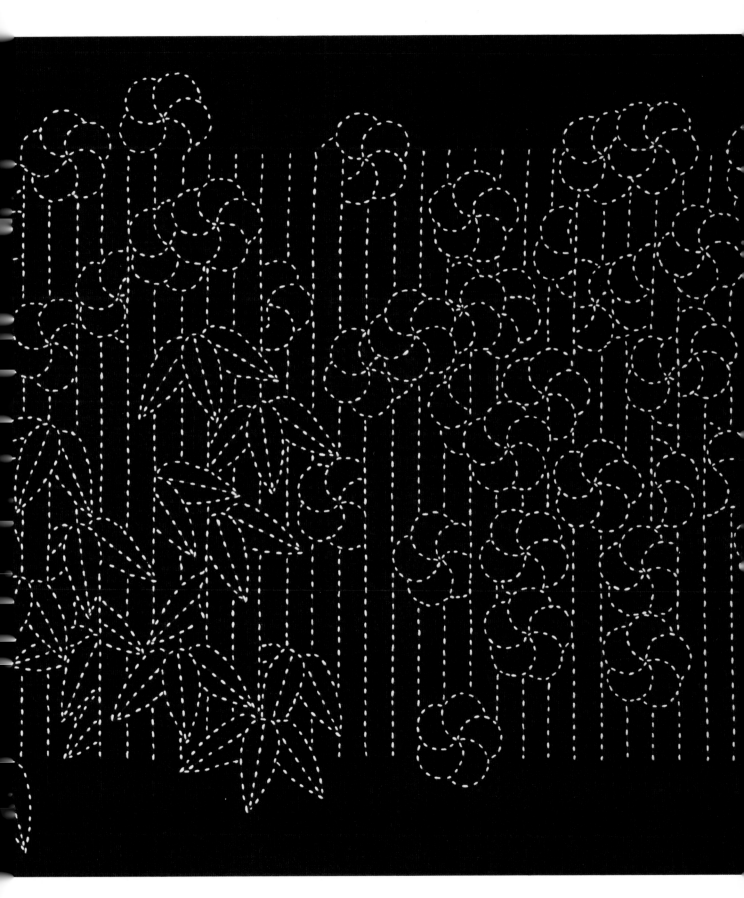

11. KARAKUSA (Arabesque pattern depicting Chinese plants)
A once-sacred symbol that has become an everyday motif

Karakusa is the Japanese name for a plant which grows in China. The arabesque pattern modeled after this plant was introduced to Japan during the Tang dynasty (618–907 A.D.), at the height of Chinese cultural influence. A wide range of objects—from tools and goods for daily use, to plants and animals, most bearing the Chinese character for "Tang" in their names—came to Japan from China during this time. However, some of the objects introduced to Japan in this period actually originated in Korea, or other foreign countries. We say that such objects "came from the Asian continent"; this refers to items introduced from Korea as well as everything which entered Japan via China, including goods originating in Greece, West Asia and India which entered China through the Middle East and the Silk Road. China's Silk Road was clearly Japan's gateway to the world as well; it's no wonder that the word "Silk Road" evokes strong feelings for Japanese.

Patterns thus introduced from other countries were usually imitated faithfully at first. However, as time went by, their forms were modified to suit the tastes of designers or to meet clients requests.

The Karakusa pattern is typical of this trend, in which the pattern continued to change as it grew more popular. The pattern, which is modeled on the shape of vines, reflects man's yearning for the eternal. In Persia, for example, grapes were the symbol of a good harvest. Thus, grapevines became the basis for a pattern which included the image of the lotus, which signifies eternal life, or the shapes of palms, which represent fertility. Such patterns were introduced to China through the Silk Road, and they became popularized during the Tang dynasty.

These patterns came to Japan with the introduction of Buddhism, and were first used to decorate the plinths supporting the images of Buddha, and on the walls of buildings. Later, in the Kamakura and Muromachi periods, new variations of the Karakusa motif arose, as designs for chinaware and woven fabrics. The pattern came to incorporate typical Japanese plants and flowers, and gradually became less and less associated with Buddhism. A Karakusa pattern composed only of curved lines and no flowers was also developed, but all the patterns were still modeled on the vine, a popular symbol of longevity and prosperity owing to its strength and continual growth. The custom of covering the furniture of newlyweds with fabric bearing the Karakusa pattern is still practiced in some areas of Japan.

Today, the Karakusa pattern is more familiar as a design seen on *furoshiki* (wrapping cloths). The furoshiki, which is basically just a large square piece of cloth, is a common household item in Japan, used to wrap anything from paper to rugby balls, regardless of its size or shape. Furoshiki typically measure 70×70 cm or 80×80 cm in size, and may be either plain or patterned. The technique of wrapping with furoshiki differs according to the shape of items to be wrapped; there are even large, sturdy cotton furoshiki for wrapping bedding and furniture. The Karakusa pattern often appears on this bigger type of furoshiki, but it is simplified and drawn with thick lines, lending a more casual and practical air than is true of normal-sized designs. Over the past ten years, the image of the Karakusa pattern has been rather degraded, since a popular comedian began using it for his costume.

The Karakusa pattern can be seen as an example of a once-holy pattern, transformed into a secular, popular design over the course of its long history.

Keko (Flower basket used in a Buddhist ceremony) with Openwork Design of Hosoge Flowers: *Kingin-To Hosoge Sukashibori Keko.*
Bronze, gold and silver plated.
Heian-Kamakura period, 12–13th century.
Jinsho-ji, Shiga.
Photograph provided by Korin-sha Shuppan.

12. KUMO & KAMINARI (Clouds and thunder)
The dragon god, a symbol of nobility and power

Patterns taken from nature include those modeled on weather phenomena, such as fog, snow, clouds and thunder.

In ancient times, it was believed that God and heavenly spirits dwelled in the sky, and clouds possessed a spiritual image. In China and in Japan, clouds were thought to be vehicles for Buddha and other celestial beings. The Kumo (cloud) pattern was thus often drawn on noblemen's vehicles, buildings and attire, and it became the symbol of rulers and authority. Later, its meaning changed: With their lofty height putting them out of reach of common people, clouds came to symbolize the Imperial Court, and nobility and others attached to the court were called *Unjobito*, or

Noh Outer Robe: *Hana-iro, Moegi, Chadan Rimpo, Inazuma, Sugikodachi-mon, Atsuita Karaori.*
Edo period, 17th century.
The Tokugawa Art Museum, Aichi.
Thunder-cloud and lightening designs in brocade weave with floating karaori-style Buddhist prayer wheels and cryptomeria trees on staggered squares of blue, light green and tan background, silk.
"Atsuita Karaori" is a thick weave using threads of gold, silver and other colors. In Noh, this is most often seen on costumes for roles which require authority and power.

66

people living on the clouds. Although the Japanese Imperial family has become more accessible to the public since the Second World War, the term Unjobito is still sometimes used. The present Empress, who was the first commoner to become Crown Princess, reportedly once joked to her close friends about her concern that "I am so fat that I will fall from the clouds."

The Kumo pattern, therefore, has been used to adorn the personal belongings and attire of people in the upper classes. The Kumo pattern with a crane is found exclusively on ceremonial costumes for the Imperial family. The present Emperor wore a costume decorated with this pattern for his coming-of-age ceremony.

Kaminari, or thunder, has always been feared due to its fierceness compared to other weather phenomena, but its role in bringing cherished rain for crops and good harvests has also embued thunderbolts with spiritual power for many. A pattern was formed from thunderbolts and it became a symbol of good harvests and heavenly power.

In ancient China, the dragon was believed to be the god of rain and the guardian of Buddha. The thunder shaking heaven and earth was thought to be the cry of a dragon in the sky, traveling freely between heaven and earth. Some Chinese art features huge snakes instead of dragons, but many paintings of dragons with clouds and lightening bolts can still be seen in shrines.

Another type of Kaminari pattern, in the form of a square coil, appears on bronze ware from China's Yin and Zhou dynasties. Found in various parts of the world, it is apparently of geometric origin. Although its relationship with clouds is unclear, this pattern is a popular motif for the chinaware of Chinese restaurants in Japan.

Both the Kumo and Kaminari patterns, with their dramatic presence, are used to symbolize power in the costumes of Noh plays.

Today the malevolent aspects of clouds and thunder seem more common, reflecting numerous people suffering throughout so many years from drought and floods.

WAVE PATTERNS

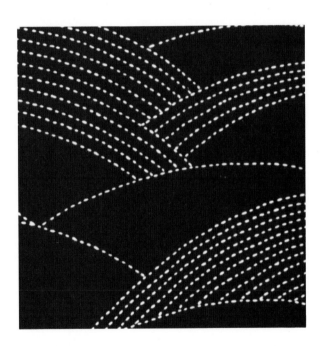

120 × 120 cm.

120 × 120 cm.

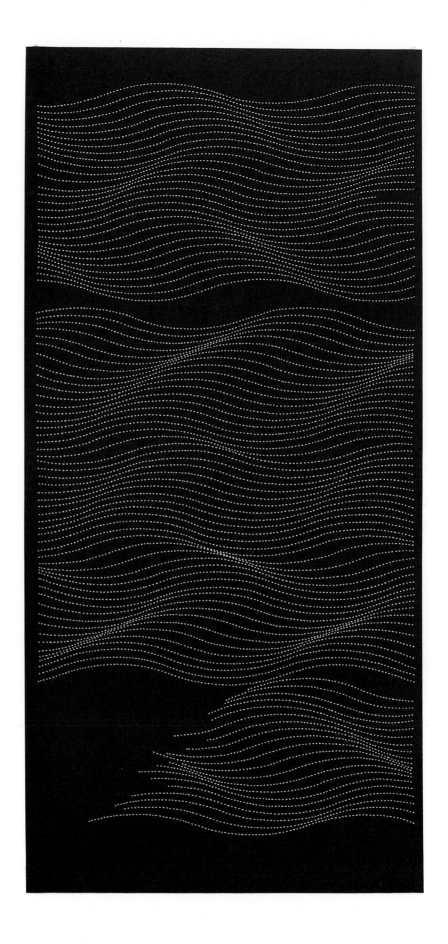

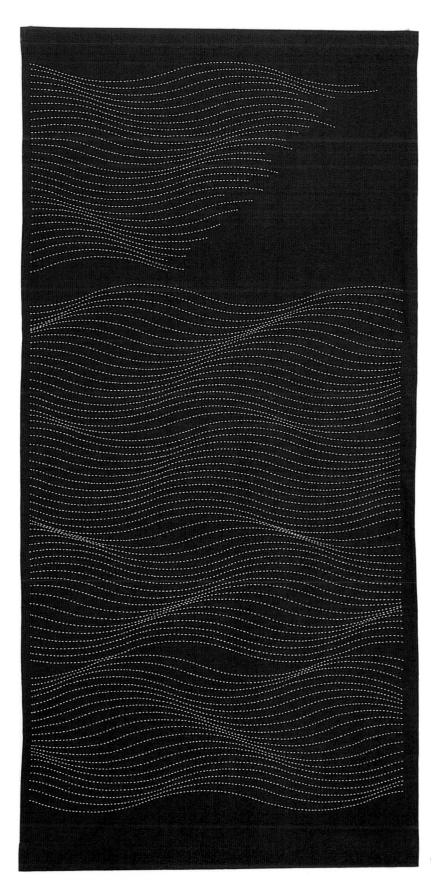

90 × 180 cm. 2 pieces.

32 × 240 cm. 5 pieces.

120 × 180 cm.

BOX PATTERNS

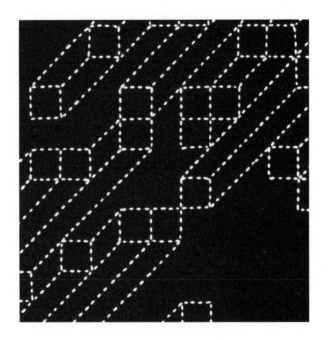

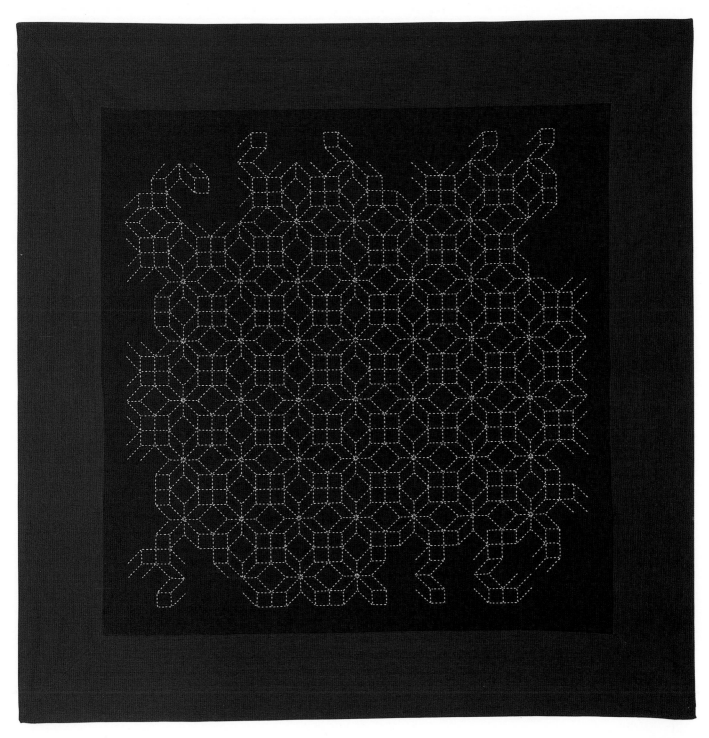

120 × 120 cm.

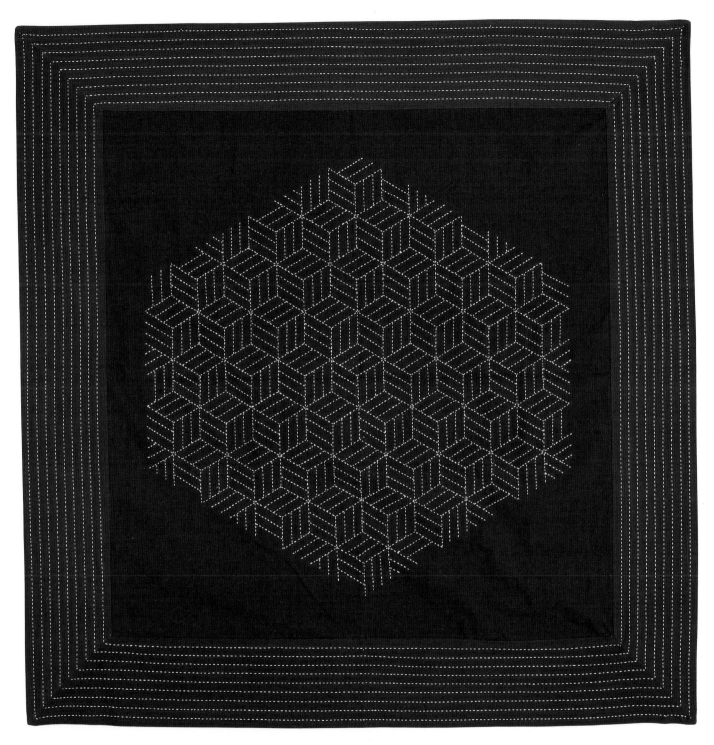

120 × 120 cm.

90 × 180 cm. 2 pieces.

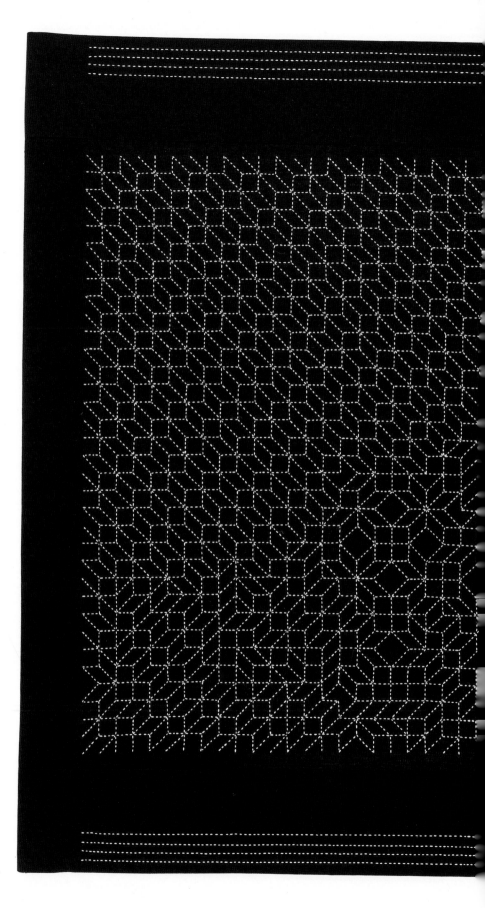

120 × 180 cm.

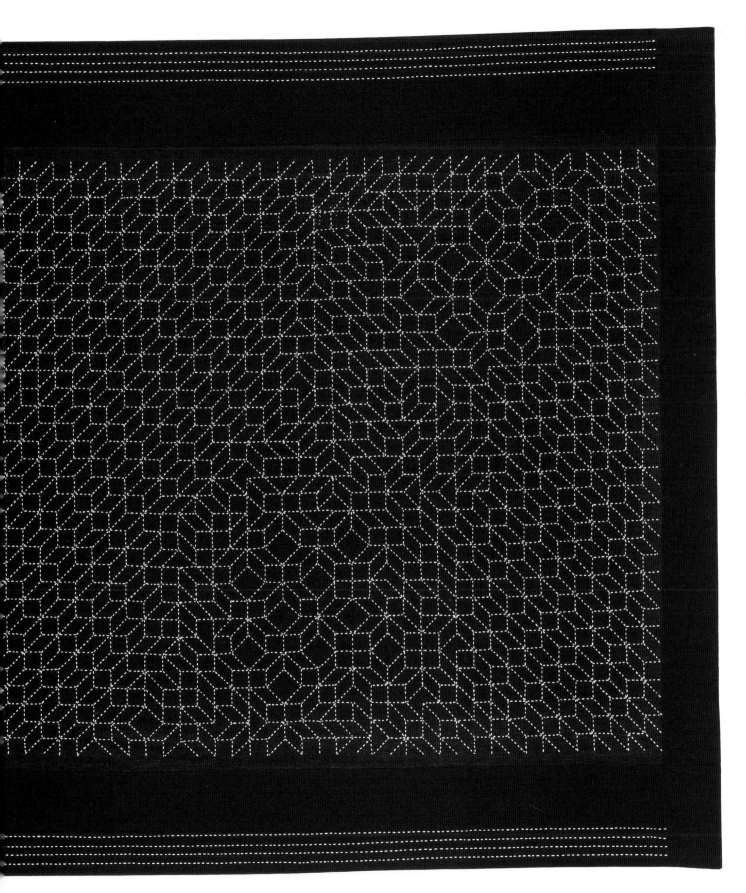

32 × 240 cm. 7 pieces.

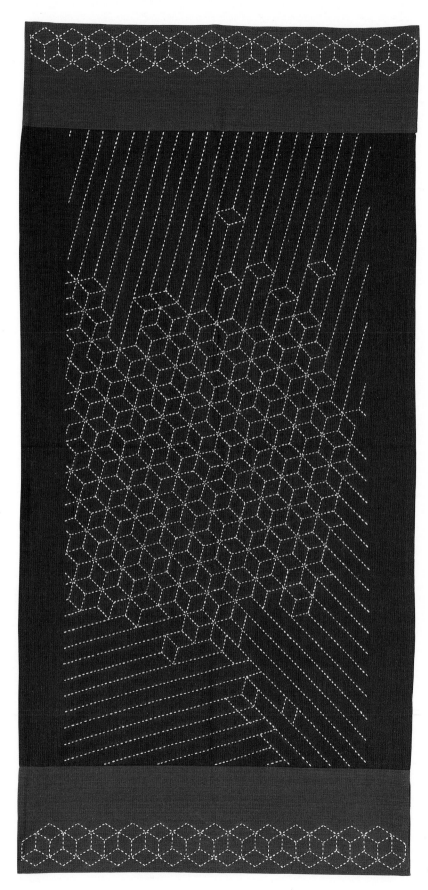

60 × 120 cm.

GEOMETRIC PATTERNS

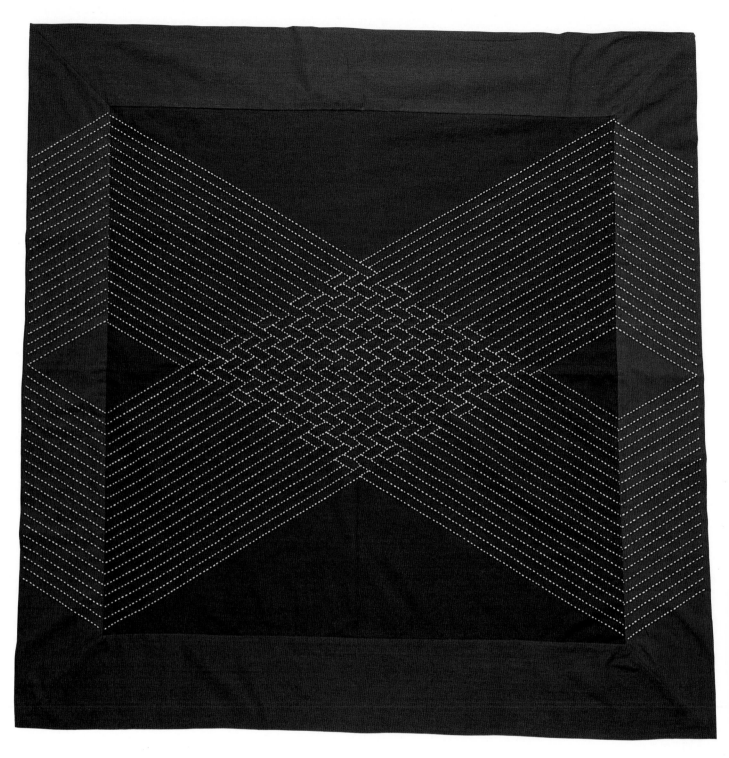

120 × 120 cm.

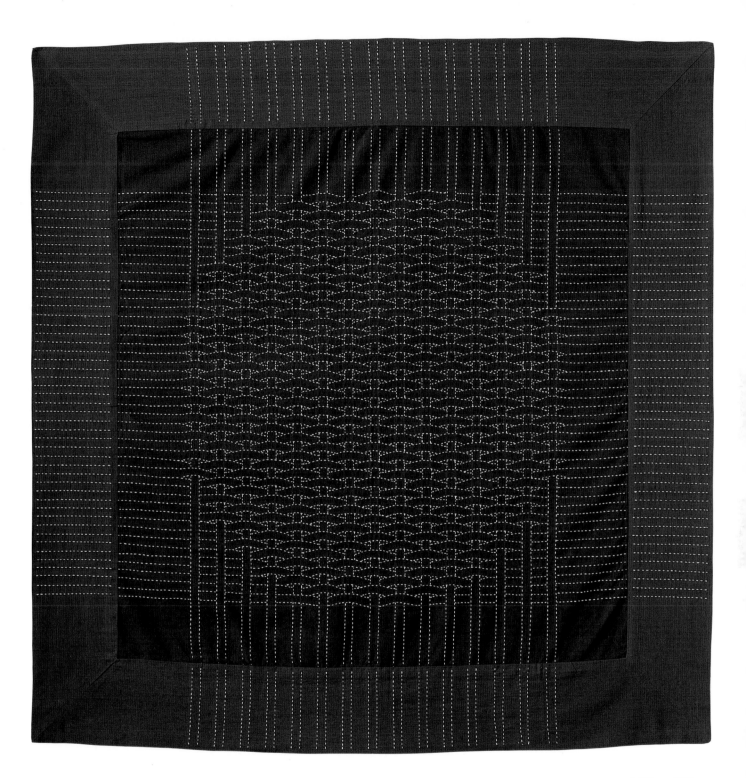

120 × 120 cm.

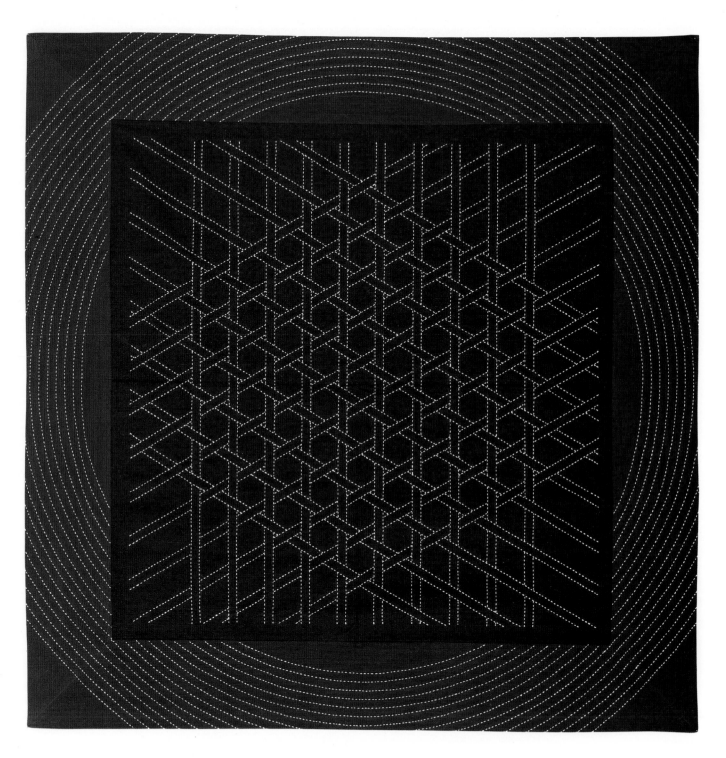

120 × 120 cm.

120 × 120 cm.

120 × 120 cm.

120 × 120 cm.

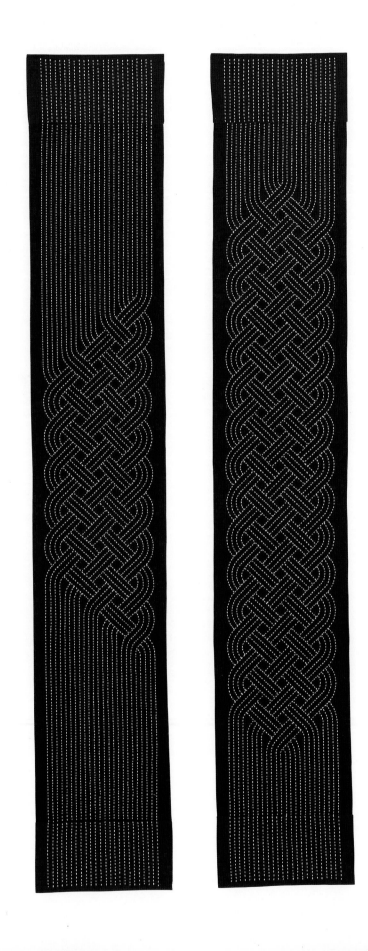

30 × 180 cm. 4 pieces.

120 × 180 cm.

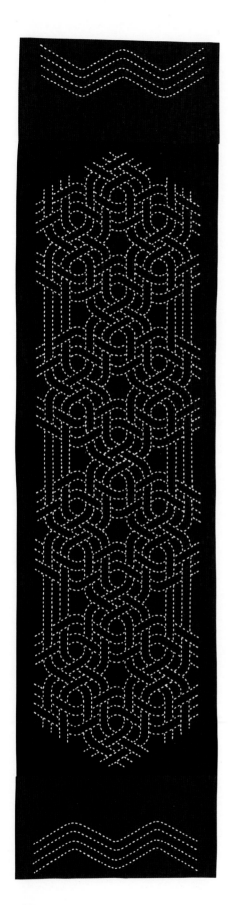
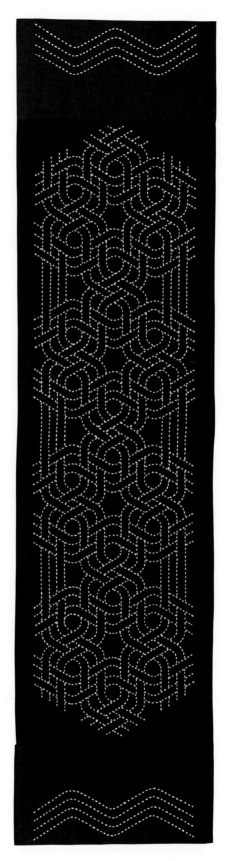

30 × 120 cm. 2 pieces.

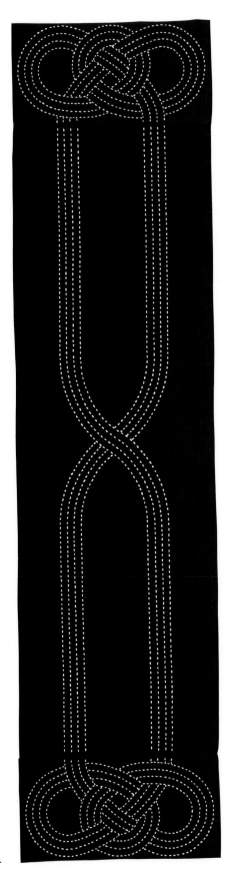
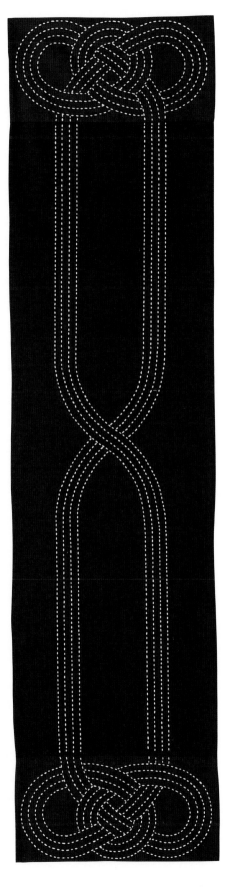

30 × 120 cm.　2 pieces.

60 × 120 cm.

ILLUSIONAL PATTERNS

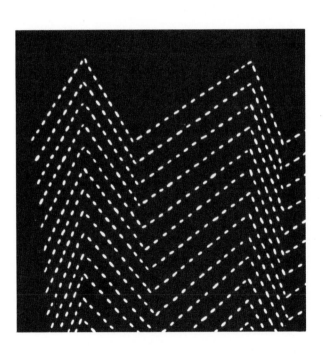

120 × 120 cm.

90 × 180 cm.

60 × 120 cm.

60 × 120 cm.

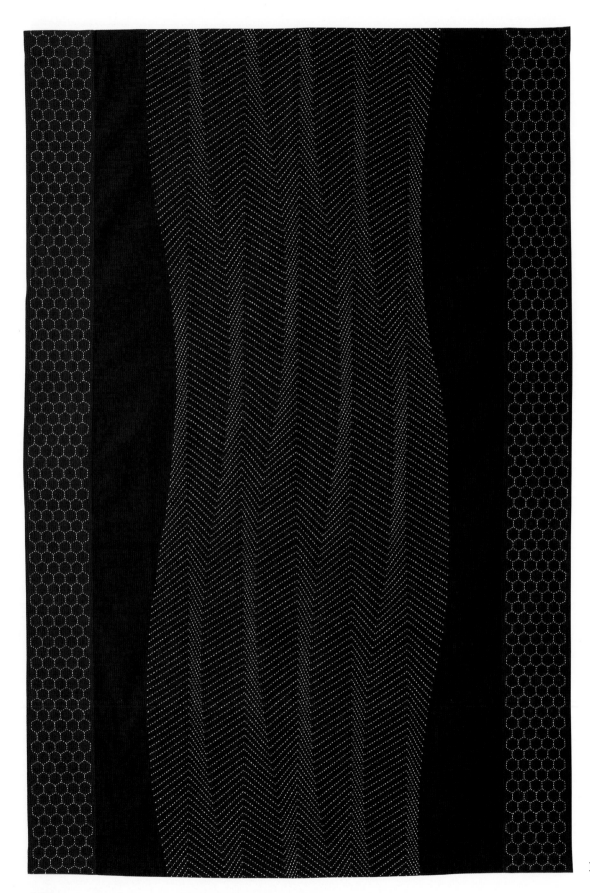

120 × 180 cm.

ART WORKS

90 × 20 cm.
Sculpture by Kyubei Kiyomizu.

20 × 210 cm. 1 piece
20 × 32 cm. 6 pieces

30 × 30 cm. 9 pieces

90 × 240 cm. 2 pieces

Artists' Profiles:

Kazuko Mende (Mrs.)

Academic Background:

1974, graduated from Women's College of Fine Arts

1976, graduated from the Master's course of Tokyo National University of Fine Arts and Music

Professional career:

Active as a teacher of drawing and design at the Women's College of Fine Arts. Also worked as a visual designer.

1980, become a partner of Morishige

Reiko Morishige (Mrs.)

Academic background:

1959, graduated from Tama University of Arts

Professional career:

1980, after working as a graphic designer, started producing her own work

Exhibitions:

1980, Tokyo, Matsuya, Asobi no Gallery, "I Love Indigo Blue"—Ideas about modern "noren" (short curtain that hangs at the entrance of a shop or room) made of "Sashiko" (quilted cloth)

1981, Tokyo, Asobi no Gallery, "Cloth in Stained Glass Design"

1983, Tokyo, Matsuya, Asobi no Gallery, "The Theme of Waves and Birds"

1985, Tokyo American Club Gallery, "Sashiko"

1986, New York, Port Washington Public Gallery, "Compositions in Indigo Blue"

1988, Tokyo, Gallery Space 21, "On Indigo Blue"

Contents: Stitchwork expressing abstract patterns using cloth in indigo blue and white thread as the materials. The artists tried to create a more inorganic space using hand-crafted materials.

Bibliography:

Encyclopedia of World Art. Shincho-sha, 1985.

Japanese Traditional Design. The Tokugawa Art Museum, 1989.

Kosode to Noh-isho. Seiroku Noma. Heibonsha Ltd.

National Treasures of Japan. The Yomiuri Shimbun, 1990.

Nihon no Monyo. Konosuke Kamijo. Yuzankaku, 1976.

Nihon no Monyo. Tetsuro Kitamura. Genryusha, 1983.

Nihon no Monyo. Korinsha Press & Co., Ltd.

Nihon no Monyo: Kacho 2, 3. Shiro Kitamura, Mitsukuni Yoshida and Ikko Tanaka. Tankosha, 1968.

Non no Design. Shozo Masuda. Heibonsha Ltd.

Monyo I, II. Asahi Shimbun Publishing Company.

Monyo no Hakubutsushi. Mitsukuni Yoshida. Dohosha Shuppann Co., Ltd., 1985.

Shosoin. Haruyuki Tono. Iwanami Shoten, 1988.

SASHIKO
Blue and White Quilt Art of Japan

SHUFUNOTOMO/JAPAN PUBLICATIONS